photography by Martin Brigdale

Quadrille
PUBLISHING

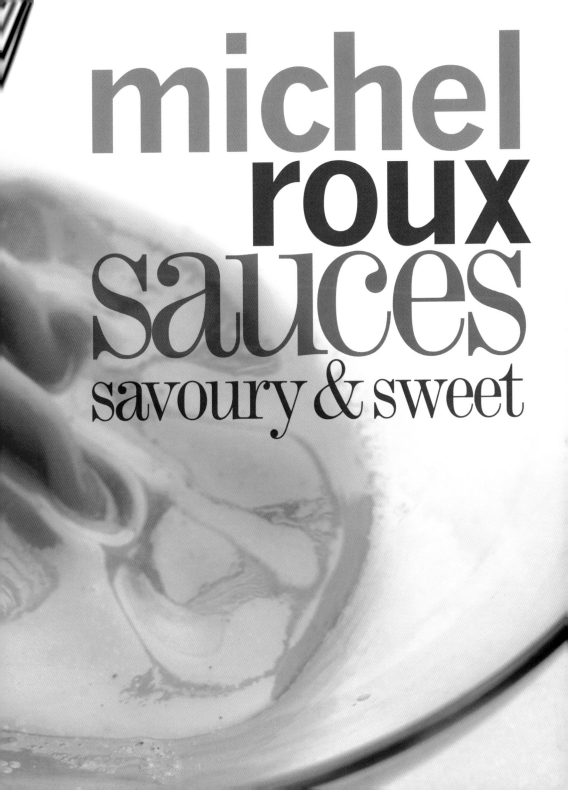

michel roux
sauces
savoury & sweet

notes

All spoon measures are level unless otherwise
stated: 1tsp = 5ml spoon; 1tbsp = 15ml spoon.

Use fresh herbs, sea salt and freshly ground
black pepper unless otherwise suggested.

Egg sizes are given where they are critical,
otherwise use medium eggs, preferably organic
or free-range. Anyone who is pregnant or in a
vulnerable health group should avoid sauces
that use raw egg whites or lightly cooked eggs.

Timings are for fan-assisted ovens. If using a
conventional oven, increase the temperature by
15°C (1 Gas mark). Use an oven thermometer
to check the temperature.

Editorial director **Anne Furniss**
Creative director **Mary Evans**
Project editor **Janet Illsley**
Translators **Sally Somers** and **Kate Whiteman**
Photographer **Martin Brigdale**
Props stylist **Helen Trent**
Production **Marina Asenjo**

First published in 2009 by
Quadrille Publishing Limited
Alhambra House
27-31 Charing Cross Road
London WC2H 0LS
www.quadrille.co.uk

Reprinted in 2009, 2010 (twice), 2011 (twice)
10 9 8 7 6

Text © 2009 Michel Roux
Photography © 2009 Martin Brigdale
Design and layout © 2009 Quadrille Publishing Limited

Cataloguing in Publication Data: a catalogue record for
this book is available from the British Library.

ISBN 978 1 84400 697 7

Printed in China

introduction

I have always compared cooking and its various disciplines to a magnificent, hundred-year-old tree – mighty, full of life and reaching out in all directions, with the trunk's sap providing nourishment to every branch. As one of the many roots of the tree – up there, or rather down there, with the grandest of them – you would undoubtedly find sauces.

I first discovered the magic of sauces as a 14-year-old apprentice to a professional chef. It was then that I learnt to master the classic sauces, which play such an important part in French cuisine. From that time onwards, I have modified and put my own stamp on all manner of sauces to best fit my own tastes, which have been in a state of continuous and subtle evolution.

It is a huge pleasure for me to revisit the first edition of my book *Sauces*, published in 1996, and so to find myself in the position of fine-tuning such a body of work, and also of sharing with you some modern sauces from all over the globe. Nages, coulis, salsas and simple jus, for example, now form part of my expanded repertoire. My contemporary sauces are aromatic, light and delicate on the palate, with a long finish in the mouth, thickened only lightly to allow their true flavours to shine through.

Sauces are the cook's alchemy, magically enhancing the dishes they are served with in an extraordinary way. They must, however be chosen carefully, so as to heighten the flavours of the dish without overpowering them in any way. A carefully prepared sauce will meld into a dish and become an integral part.

Martin Brigdale's superb step-by-step photographs at the start of each chapter will make it easy for you to master the techniques. Sauce-making is a wonderfully creative and expressive branch of cooking… I hope this new volume will inspire you to explore it to the full.

You need very little in the way of special equipment for sauce-making and you are likely to have most of the essential items in your kitchen already. The following are particularly useful.

Whisks, spatulas and spoons A classic long-handled metal whisk with an easy-to-grip handle is essential for many sauces, not least emulsions, such as hollandaise and mayonnaise, and sabayons. A hand-held electric whisk is a labour-saving option, although I prefer to use a hand whisk for most tasks. You will also need a wooden spatula and a long-handled wooden spoon for stirring sauces over heat.

Blenders A free-standing electric blender is useful for puréeing, although for most sauces, I find a hand-held stick blender more convenient as it can be used directly in the pan or bowl you are preparing the sauce in. It purées and emulsifies sauces, aerating them at the same time to make them light and frothy. I use Krups blenders in my kitchen – the hand blender and free-standing model are both easy to use and very efficient.

Strainers and sieves For sauces, a conical strainer made of perforated metal, known as a chinois, is useful. For most purposes, however, you will need a fine-meshed sieve. A conical wire-meshed sieve, known as a chinois fin, is the easiest type to use for straining sauces and stocks. If you do not have one already, I strongly recommend you buy one of these. I also find a wooden drum sieve useful for savoury butters.

Pots and pans Good-quality saucepans are essential to enable sauces to be cooked to perfection. Buying a good set of durable pans is probably the best investment you can make for your kitchen, as they will last a lifetime. I use All-clad pans, which give excellent results. For stock-making, stainless steel stockpots and deep, heavy-based saucepans have replaced the huge copper stockpots I used for many years.

Other items You will also need a set of weighing scales, measuring spoons, a measuring jug, a zester, a ladle, a large metal spoon, a skimming spoon, a plastic spatula, Pyrex mixing bowls of various sizes (suitable for placing over a pan of simmering water) and a cooking thermometer for testing the temperature of sauces such as sabayons.

basic elements

All sauces, however simple or complex, must be based on good-quality ingredients. Aromatics, fresh herbs, vegetables, spices, wine and other alcohol, stocks and fumets – all must be chosen with quality and freshness in mind. As far as possible, use produce in season.

Stocks These are the very foundation of sauces. The quality of the stock you use will determine the success of your sauce. The great classics, in particular, rely on fine homemade stocks. Recipes for all of the stocks you will need for the sauces in this book are given in the following chapter.

Butter I use butter in many of my sauces, but always in moderation. It adds an important finishing touch to so many classics. The delicate and different complexities of butter vary according to its provenance and origins, but unsalted is my preferred choice for cooking. Unsalted butter is essential for making clarified butter and desirable for all sauces in my opinion. French echiré is my favourite.

Flour White flour is used together with butter to make a roux – the thickener for all white sauces, including veloutés. I like to use a good-quality organic plain flour. As humidity has an adverse effect on flour, always store it in a dry place, transferring it to an airtight container once you have opened the packet.

Eggs Egg yolks are an essential ingredient in mayonnaise, hollandaise and most other emulsion sauces. They are also used to make crème anglaise and other custard-type sauces. Most of these sauces are prepared with raw or lightly cooked egg yolks, so it is essential that they are very, very fresh. Always use good-quality organic or free-range eggs.

Double cream I use cream to enrich sauces and give them a velvety texture, though in general I add rather less to my recipes than I did a decade ago, as I now prefer my sauces to have a lighter texture. Double cream tolerates heat well and sauces can be reduced by boiling after it has been added.

Crème fraîche With its mild acidity, this adds a light creaminess and lively, fresh taste to cold sauces and dressings. Once added to sauces, they can be heated to about 80°C but should not be boiled otherwise the crème fraîche is liable to separate.

Cheeses Parmesan, Gruyère, medium Cheddar and Roquefort are the cheeses I use most often to flavour sauces, dressings and savoury butters. After a cheese has been added to a sauce it takes a few minutes for their savour to develop, so add judiciously at first, checking after a few minutes before adding more. Season sauces after adding cheese, not before.

All manner of flavouring ingredients can be used to add character to savoury and sweet sauces, but they should always be chosen carefully and used in moderation – especially pungent spices, garlic and chillies – to ensure they do not become overpowering.

Herbs These play a vital role in sauce-making, imparting subtle flavours, complexity and freshness. The herbs most often used to flavour sauces and dressings are basil, bay leaf, chervil, chives, coriander, dill, fennel, lemon grass, mint, parsley, rosemary, sage, savory, sorrel, tarragon and thyme.
Fines herbes is a mixture of fresh chervil, chives, parsley and tarragon in equal quantities. The herbs should be snipped, not chopped, preferably shortly before adding to retain maximum flavour and freshness.
Bouquet garni is a bundle of herbs added to a sauce to flavour it during cooking and then removed. A classic bouquet garni consists of a sprig of thyme, a bay leaf, parsley stalks and a leek leaf. To make the bouquet, wrap the herbs in the leek leaf and tie securely with string.

Spices The most popular spices for use in sauces are caraway, cardamom, cayenne, cinnamon, cloves, coriander seeds, cumin, curry, five-spice, ginger, juniper berries, mace, nutmeg, black, green and white peppercorns, paprika, pimento, poppy seeds, saffron and star anise. They should all be used sparingly. To obtain the maximum flavour when using saffron threads, pound them in a mortar or crush them with your fingertips into the palm of your hand, then infuse them in a little warm water.

Seasoning Always use good-quality sea salt and freshly ground pepper. To avoid the possibility of over-seasoning, add salt to a sauce sparingly before it has reached the desired consistency, then taste and adjust the salt at the end. Add pepper only just before serving to retain its flavour and zip.

Garlic This is used to flavour dressings and certain sauces, such as sauce vierge and pistou. Always halve garlic cloves lengthways and remove the central germ, which can be indigestible. To crush garlic, I put the halved cloves in a mortar with a good pinch of coarse salt and crush the garlic to a paste with the pestle.

Chillies These add heat to salsas and piquant sauces. Generally the smaller the chilli the hotter it is – habanero chillies are among the hottest – and the hottest part of any chilli is nearest to the stem. The most commonly used chillies are jalapeño, serrano and poblano. As chilli is an irritant, it is important to wash your hands immediately after handling, or better still, wear disposable gloves as you prepare them.

Vinegar and lemon juice A few drops added at the last moment will add a little character to a sauce that is a bit on the 'thin' side. Note that adding either to a roux-based sauce will loosen it slightly.

whisking sauces

Whisking is an important technique in sauce-making, used to emulsify and mix sauces smoothly. Using a balloon whisk rather than an electric whisk gives you more control and makes it easier to stop whisking at precisely the right stage. Hold the whisk comfortably in your hand and rotate the wrist, using a light, rapid motion.

When making an emulsion sauce like mayonnaise (recipe on pages 82–3), whisk constantly as you add the oil – very slowly to begin with, then in a trickle.

Using a blender is an effective
way of puréeing sauces, such as fruit
and vegetable coulis like the asparagus
coulis shown here (recipe on page 156),
to give a smooth-textured result. Whiz using a
hand-held stick blender (or free-standing one) for
2–5 minutes, depending on how aerated you want the
sauce to be. Sauces will froth up when emulsified with a
hand blender so be sure to use a deep enough saucepan.

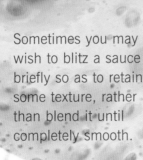

Sometimes you may
wish to blitz a sauce
briefly so as to retain
some texture, rather
than blend it until
completely smooth.

thickening sauces

A roux is the classic way to thicken many classic French sauces. It is a mixture of equal quantities of melted butter and flour stirred together and cooked (as described below) before any liquid is added.

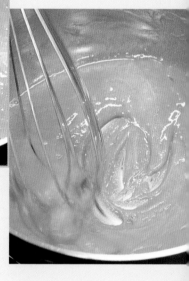

White roux This is used for all white sauces. The roux is cooked, stirring, over a medium heat for about 2 minutes.

Blond roux This pale roux is used for veloutés and sauces where a neutral colour is needed – for poultry, for example. The roux is cooked, stirring, over a medium heat for about 4 minutes until pale hazelnut brown in colour.

Brown roux This is used to thicken many brown sauces. Use clarified butter for the roux and cook it for about 8 minutes, stirring continuously, until it turns chestnut brown in colour.

Beyond the basic roux, thickening agents rarely feature in my sauces nowadays, as lighter sauces achieved by natural reduction are better suited to today's tastes. However, the following have certain specific uses.

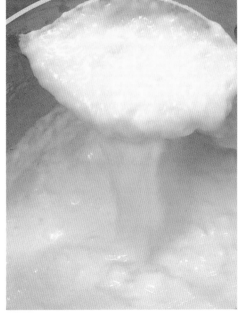

Cornflour and arrowroot These are quick and easy to use. Simply blend with a little cold milk or water and stir into the hot sauce at the end of cooking. Stir over the heat for 2–3 minutes to cook out the floury taste.

Bread Fresh breadcrumbs are used to thicken the classic English bread sauce (shown above), traditionally served with roast poultry and game. They also thicken rustic sauces, such as the Spanish Romesco.

reductions

Reducing sauces by boiling intensifies their flavour, thickening and enriching them. Demi-glace and glace sauces are made by reducing strained stocks down, skimming from time to time. At each stage the sauce has a distinct texture.

Initially, boiling over high heat will reduce veal stock to a light jus (shown left).

Further reduction to about one-third of the original volume produces a darker, slightly syrupy sauce – a demi-glace (recipe on pages 26–7).

A demi-glace can be reduced further to a very thick, rich, sticky glace. Here the thickness is visible on the spoon and across the base of the pan.

Many sauces are reduced gently until they reach the desired consistency. Initially the basic stock or other liquor may be concentrated. After wine or other alcohol is added, it is invariably reduced. If a sauce is enriched with cream, further light reduction may be required.

As a stock reduces, impurities rise to the surface, which should be skimmed off.

If cream is added to a sauce, it can be reduced by gentle bubbling (as for seafood sauce with saffron, shown above (recipe on page 188).

You should be able to judge by eye when a sauce has reached the desired consistency, but you can always run your finger down the back of the spoon to check it.

Almost any sauce can be given added richness and shine at the end by 'mounting with butter', or adding cream or a liason of egg yolks.

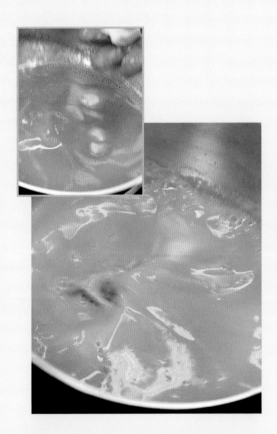

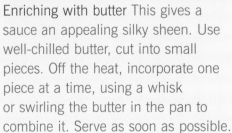

Enriching with butter This gives a sauce an appealing silky sheen. Use well-chilled butter, cut into small pieces. Off the heat, incorporate one piece at a time, using a whisk or swirling the butter in the pan to combine it. Serve as soon as possible.

Enriching with cream This adds a velvety richness to fish and chicken veloutés, and many other sauces. Double cream should always be used. Some sauces, such as a mousseline, are enriched and lightened by folding in lightly whipped cream at the end.

Enriching with eggs Sauces bound with egg yolks have a velvety texture and delicate colour. First break up the egg yolks in a bowl with a little liquid (at room temperature) – milk, cream, chicken stock, etc. depending on the sauce. Off the heat, pour into the hot sauce, whisking constantly. Return to a low heat and reheat the sauce, whisking continuously; don't let it boil or it will separate. This is a way to thicken sauces at the last minute.

The easiest way to
strain a sauce to obtain
a silky, smooth result is to
pass it through a fine-meshed
conical sieve. Thicker sauces can
be pushed through by pressing down
with the back of a ladle or wooden spoon.

Most sauces are best served soon after making. If you need to keep a sauce warm for a short while, use a bain-marie. You can buy one (see left) or simply fill a saucepan – large enough to hold the pan or bowl containing the sauce – with hot water and stand the bowl in the pan. Dot flakes of butter over the surface of white sauces to prevent a skin from forming and cover with cling film or a lid. If a sauce is to be finished with butter, do this just before serving.

clarifying butter

This is used for emulsified sauces like hollandaise and its derivatives.

To make about 100g clarified butter, you will need 120g unsalted butter.

Melt the butter over a very gentle heat and bring slowly to the boil. Skim off the froth from the surface. Carefully pour the liquid butter into a bowl, holding back the milky sediment in the bottom of pan. The clarified butter should be the colour of light olive oil. It will keep in the fridge for a couple of weeks.

Nowadays, we like our stocks to be light so that our sauces are subtle, delicate, almost balletic. It is essential that all the ingredients for a stock – vegetables, meat bones, carcasses, fish bones, etc. – are perfectly fresh and of top quality. Add just enough cold water to barely cover the ingredients and, during cooking, top up with a little more cold water as necessary to ensure that the stock remains crystal clear. Follow the cooking time suggested in each recipe precisely, to extract the optimum flavour. Stocks will keep well in an airtight container in the fridge for up to 5 days, or they can be frozen for up to a month. Freeze in convenient quantities and don't forget to label and date the containers as you will find it difficult to identify them once frozen. As for marinades, the purpose of these is to tenderise poultry, meats, game and fish, and to penetrate the flesh with their distinctive flavours. There are many options, but in general, marinades are designed to suit different foods, so some are better suited to red meat and game, some to poultry, while others work best with fish or shellfish. A few spoonfuls of the respective marinade can be added to a game sauce to enhance the flavour; or to a roasting pan when deglazing to intensify the flavour of the jus.

stocks & marinades

veal stock

makes 1 litre

Veal stock forms the base for almost all brown sauces, and is often used in fish sauces as well.

1.5kg veal bones, chopped
½ calf's foot, split lengthways, chopped
   and blanched for 5 minutes
200g carrots, cut into rounds
100g onion, coarsely chopped
250ml dry white wine

1 celery stalk, thinly sliced
6 tomatoes, peeled, deseeded and chopped
150g button mushrooms, thinly sliced
2 garlic cloves
1 bouquet garni, including 1 tarragon sprig

Preheat the oven to 220°C/Gas 7. Put the veal bones and calf's foot in a roasting pan and roast in the oven for about 40 minutes, turning them from time to time with a slotted spoon, until well browned. Add the carrots and onion, mix together and cook for another 5 minutes.

Using the slotted spoon, transfer the entire contents of the roasting pan to a large saucepan or casserole. Pour off the fat from the roasting pan and deglaze with the white wine, scraping up all the sediment. Set over a high heat and reduce by half, then pour the wine into the saucepan.

Add 3 litres cold water and bring to the boil over a high heat. As soon as the liquid boils, reduce the heat so that the surface is barely trembling. Simmer very gently for 10 minutes, then skim well.

Add all the other ingredients and simmer the stock, uncovered, for 2 ¹/₂ hours, skimming as necessary. Strain through a fine-meshed or muslin-lined conical strainer into a bowl and cool over ice. Refrigerate and use within 4 or 5 days, or freeze for up to 3 months.

demi-glace/glace Reduce the strained stock by one-third to make a demi-glace; reduce by half for a glace. These glaces enhance sauces, lending a fuller flavour, but they cannot add finesse and subtlety, since the lengthy cooking time involved destroys some of their delicate flavour and aroma.

makes about 1.5 litres

This stock has many uses in the kitchen. I sometimes add half a knuckle of veal when preparing it, to make it extra rich and unctuous.

1 boiling fowl, weighing 1.5kg, or an equal
weight of raw chicken carcasses or wings,
blanched and refreshed
200g carrots, cut into chunks
2 leeks, white part only, cut into chunks

1 celery stalk, coarsely chopped
1 onion, studded with 2 cloves
150g button mushrooms, thinly sliced
1 bouquet garni

Put the chicken or carcasses into a saucepan and cover with 2.5 litres cold water. Bring to the boil over a high heat, then immediately lower the heat and keep at a simmer.

After 5 minutes, skim the surface and add all the other ingredients. Cook gently for $1^1/_2$ hours, without boiling, skimming whenever necessary.

Strain the stock through a fine-meshed conical sieve into a bowl and cool over ice. Refrigerate and use within 4 or 5 days, or freeze for up to 3 months.

Stocks – and sauces that cook slowly – should be skimmed from time to time. This is best carried out with a spoon or small skimmer, in order to remove any bits, impurities and fats floating on the surface of the liquid.

illustrated on page 25

This stock is light in both flavour and appearance. I use it for deglazing in many roast or pan-fried lamb recipes, such as a navarin.

1.5kg scrag end, breast or lower best end of
  lamb, skin and fat removed
150g carrots, cut into rounds
100g onions, coarsely chopped
250ml dry white wine

4 tomatoes, peeled, deseeded and chopped
2 garlic cloves
1 bouquet garni, including 2 tarragon sprigs
  and a celery stalk
6 white peppercorns, crushed

Preheat the oven to 220°C/Gas 7. Cut the lamb into pieces and place in a roasting pan. Brown in the hot oven, turning the pieces over from time to time with a slotted spoon, for about 20 minutes. When the lamb has coloured, add the carrots and onions, mix together and cook for another 5 minutes.

Using the slotted spoon, transfer the contents of the roasting pan to a large saucepan or casserole. Pour off the fat from the roasting pan, deglaze with the white wine and reduce by half.

Pour the reduced wine into the pan, add 2.5 litres cold water and bring to the boil over a high heat. As soon as the liquid boils, reduce the heat so that the surface is barely trembling. Simmer for 10 minutes, skim and add all the other ingredients.

Simmer, uncovered, for 1½ hours, skimming the surface as necessary. Strain the stock through a fine-meshed conical sieve into a bowl and cool over ice. Refrigerate and use within 4 or 5 days, or freeze for up to 3 months.

If I am making this stock to form the basis for a sauce, I flavour it with curry, star anise, mint or saffron to complement the particular dish. It is also perfect for moistening a couscous garnished with tender young vegetables.

fish stock or fumet

makes 2 litres

Fish stock is used in various sauces to accompany fish.
If it is intended for a red wine sauce, use red rather than white wine.

1.5kg white fish bones and trimmings (from
   sole, turbot, brill, whiting, etc.), cut into pieces
50g butter
2 leeks, white part only, thinly sliced
75g onions, thinly sliced

75g button mushrooms, thinly sliced
200ml dry white wine
1 bouquet garni
2 lemon slices
8 white peppercorns, crushed and tied in muslin

Rinse the fish bones and trimmings under cold running water, then drain. Melt the
butter in a large saucepan, add the sliced vegetables and sweat over a low heat for
a few minutes.

Add the fish bones and trimmings and allow to bubble gently for a few moments,
then pour in the white wine. Cook until it has reduced by two-thirds, then add
2.5 litres cold water. Bring to the boil, lower the heat, skim the surface and add
the bouquet garni and lemon slices.

Simmer very gently for 25 minutes, skimming as necessary. About 10 minutes
before the end of cooking, add the muslin-wrapped peppercorns.

Gently ladle the stock through a fine-meshed conical sieve into a bowl and cool
over ice. Refrigerate and use within 2 or 3 days, or freeze for up to 3 months.

Cooking a stock for longer does not make it better – quite the reverse.
With long cooking, a stock becomes heavy and loses its savour; this
applies particularly to fish stocks, which can also acquire a bitter taint.

game stock

makes 1.5 litres

This stock makes an ideal sauce for pan-fried venison.
Deglaze the pan with port, add 1 tsp redcurrant jelly, then the game stock.
Whisk in a knob of butter, season and serve.

3 tbsp groundnut oil
2kg furred or feathered game trimmings,
  carcasses, necks, wings, etc., cut into pieces
150g carrots, cut into rounds
150g onions, coarsely chopped
½ head of garlic (unpeeled), halved widthways

500ml red wine (preferably Côtes du Rhône)
500ml veal stock (page 26)
8 juniper berries, crushed
8 coriander seeds, crushed
1 bouquet garni, including 2 sage leaves
  and a celery stalk

Preheat the oven to 220°C/Gas 7. Heat the oil in a roasting pan, then put in the game carcasses or trimmings and brown in the hot oven for about 30 minutes, turning them from time to time with a slotted spoon. When the meat has browned, add the carrots, onions and garlic, mix together and cook for another 5 minutes.

With the slotted spoon, transfer all the contents of the roasting pan to a large saucepan or casserole. Pour off the fat from the roasting pan and deglaze with the red wine. Set over a high heat and reduce the wine by half, then pour it into the saucepan.

Add 2 litres cold water and bring to the boil over a high heat. As soon as the liquid boils, reduce the heat so that the surface barely trembles. Simmer for 10 minutes, then skim well and add all the other ingredients.

Simmer the stock, uncovered, for 2 hours, skimming the surface as necessary. Strain it through a fine-meshed conical sieve into a bowl and cool over ice.

Once the stock has been strained, you can reduce it by one-third to give it more body. Like all stocks, it will keep well for several days in the fridge, or for up to 4 months in the freezer.

makes 1.5 litres

300g carrots, cut into rounds
2 leeks, white part only, thinly sliced
100g celery stalks, thinly sliced
50g fennel bulb, very thinly sliced
150g shallots, thinly sliced
100g onion, thinly sliced
2 unpeeled garlic cloves
1 bouquet garni
250ml dry white wine
10 white peppercorns, crushed and
   tied in muslin

Put all the ingredients except the peppercorns in a saucepan and add 2 litres cold water. Bring to the boil over a high heat, then lower the heat and cook at a bare simmer for 45 minutes, skimming as necessary. After 35 minutes, add the muslin-wrapped peppercorns.

Strain through a fine-meshed conical sieve into a bowl and cool over ice. Refrigerate and use within 4 or 5 days, or freeze for up to 3 months.

You can substitute or add your own choice of seasonal vegetables, varying the stock with flavourful, ripe tomatoes in summer, a few wild mushrooms in autumn (chanterelles add a particularly fine aroma), and so on. Cooling a hot stock over a bowl filled with ice cubes is an effective way to cool it quickly before storing in the fridge or freezer.

orange and dill marinade for seafood

makes enough to marinate 6 portions

An instant marinade that effectively 'cooks' the raw fish it is applied to, while maintaining its raw freshness and flavour.

juice of 3 oranges
juice of 1 lemon
75ml light, fruity olive oil
20g dill fronds, finely snipped
sea salt (preferably Maldon)
freshly ground or cracked peppercorns (preferably white)

Combine all the ingredients in a bowl and mix with a spoon. Cover with cling film and leave to infuse for at least 10 minutes before using.

Spoon the marinade over thin slices of ultra-fresh raw salmon or scallops 5 minutes before serving. Garnish with a few baby salad leaves.

illustrated on previous page

makes enough to marinate 6 portions

These Asian flavours work well with prawns and langoustines. Use tongs
or a fork to turn them in the marinade and remove them after marinating.

50ml kecap manis (sweet soy)
50ml grapeseed oil
1 tbsp runny honey
1 tbsp sesame oil
60g piece of fresh root ginger, peeled and
    sliced into thin discs
10g coriander leaves, chopped

Put all the ingredients into a bowl and mix with a spoon. Cover the bowl with cling
film and leave to infuse for at least an hour.

Pour the marinade over shelled langoustines or peeled prawns. Leave to marinate
for 20 minutes before grilling or briefly pan-frying them over a high heat.

Cook the crustaceans for no more than 1 or 2 minutes, depending
on their size, to keep them moist.

sweet sour marinade for fish

makes enough to marinate 6 portions

100g caster sugar
120ml lemon juice
2 small liquorice sticks, lightly crushed
4 star anise

Pour 400ml cold water into a saucepan, add the sugar and lemon juice and slowly bring to the boil, stirring to dissolve the sugar. Toss in the liquorice sticks and star anise and simmer for 1 minute.

To use, pour the hot marinade over the fish and leave to cool to room temperature, then marinate in the refrigerator for a further 2–3 hours.

This piquant marinade is ideal for oily fish, such as mackerel, as it helps to cut the richness.

30g butter
2 carrots, cut into rounds
2 small onions, coarsely chopped
2 celery stalks, thinly sliced
1 litre red wine (preferably Côtes du Rhône)
100ml red wine vinegar
1 large bouquet garni, including a
   rosemary sprig

1 small head of garlic (unpeeled), halved
   widthways
a few mace blades, or a good pinch of
   ground mace
2 cloves
½ tsp crushed peppercorns

Melt the butter in a saucepan over a low heat. Add the vegetables and sweat gently for 5 minutes to soften slightly.

Pour in 750ml water and add all the other ingredients. Bring to the boil over a high heat, then lower the heat and simmer gently for 20 minutes, skimming the surface as necessary.

Leave to cool, then strain the marinade through a fine-meshed sieve and keep in the fridge until ready to marinate your meat. Use within a few days.

The amount of marinade you will need and the marinating time is determined by the size of the meat. For example, a leg of lamb will need about 12 hours in the marinade, while a fillet of venison will need only 2–3 hours. Put the meat in a non-metal container that will hold it and enough marinade to cover it generously. Always use a fork or tongs when handling meat in a marinade rather than your fingers, which could adversely affect the flavour.

ginger and soy marinade for red meats

makes enough to marinate 6 portions

4 garlic cloves, finely chopped
80g piece of fresh root ginger, finely grated
4 tbsp light olive oil
4 tbsp soy sauce
finely grated zest of 2 oranges

Put all the ingredients into a bowl and mix with a spoon. Cover the bowl with cling film and leave to infuse for at least 2 hours.

To apply the marinade, put on disposable gloves and massage the pieces of meat with the marinade, then place in a shallow dish, pour on the remaining marinade and cover with cling film; or place all in a plastic bag and seal it.

Leave the meat to marinate in the fridge for 6–12 hours, taking it out an hour before cooking to bring it to room temperature.

This marinade is ideal for red meats that are to be grilled or barbecued. The quantity is sufficient to marinate three 600g ribs of beef or three 500g thick rump steaks, or 6 fairly thick pork chops – helping to make them deliciously succulent.

spiced marinade for poultry

makes enough to marinate 4 portions

- 60g piece of fresh root ginger, chopped
- 2 thick chives
- 4 garlic cloves, peeled
- juice of 2 lemons
- 2 tbsp coriander leaves
- 2 tbsp sesame oil
- 2 tbsp groundnut oil
- 2 tbsp ground coriander
- 1 tbsp ground cumin
- 1 tsp chilli powder
- 1 tbsp paprika
- 1 tbsp fine salt

Put all the ingredients into a blender and blitz to a smooth paste for 2–3 minutes. Transfer to a bowl, cover with cling film and refrigerate until ready to use.

Chicken or turkey breasts and thighs really benefit from 6–12 hours in this marinade. Thereafter, they can simply be steamed, then briefly pan-fried in clarified butter just before serving to crisp up the skin.

Light, fragrant and refreshing, the recipes in this chapter could not be more diet-conscious, especially the infusions. These simple yet sublime 'aromatic waters' are perfect with steamed or poached fish, shellfish and poultry. According to the season and your taste, feel free to substitute or add fresh herbs and julienne vegetables to your infusion. Tomato water, one of my favourites, is simply the natural water from the fruit packed with all the savours of tomato. Grated cucumber and other vegetables with a high water content will disgorge their natural water to give the same result. I like to serve these waters chilled in a small cup at the start of a meal to refresh the palate. Quick to prepare, nages are a little saucier – closer to a light sauce in fact. In the final stage of their preparation, I add a little butter and sometimes even a touch of cream…

infusions & nages

serves 6

1.5kg very ripe plum tomatoes (preferably Roma)
10 basil leaves
1 thyme sprig
30g sea salt (preferably Maldon)

Blitz all the ingredients in a food processor or blender until the tomatoes are very finely chopped.

Line a sieve with a double layer of muslin and set it over a bowl. Tip the chopped tomatoes into the sieve. Place in the fridge for about 6 hours, until the 'tomato water' has dripped through into the bowl. Do not be tempted to force it through otherwise the liquid will lose its clarity. Keep the tomato water and discard the pulp.

Tomato water should be as clear as spring water. You can heat it if you wish, but don't let the temperature exceed 70°C, or it will turn cloudy. It will keep in an airtight container in the fridge for up to 3 days.

I like to serve tomato water as a consommé garnished with seafood or tiny vegetables, such as baby broad beans or peas.

aromatic herb infusion

serves 6

6 sage leaves
3 thyme sprigs
6 fennel or dill fronds
2 lemon grass stalks
2 tarragon stems
6 mint leaves
finely pared zest of 1 lemon

Bring 2 litres water to the boil in a saucepan, then add all the herbs and the lemon zest. Turn off the heat and put a lid on the saucepan. Leave to infuse for 3–4 minutes.

Strain the infusion through a conical strainer into the base of a steamer. It is now ready to steam your fish.

White fish, such as cod, pollack and whiting, all benefit from steaming over this herb infusion, which imparts a subtle aroma to the delicate flesh.

illustrated on page 45

serves 6–8

I discovered this extraordinary Parmesan water some years ago
at Annie Féolde's renowned Enoteca Pinchiorri in Florence, where
she served it in little glasses as a divine amuse-bouche.
I sometimes garnish it with tiny sage-flavoured potato gnocchi.

**250g best-quality Parmigiano-Reggiano,
  aged for at least 1 year, finely diced
freshly ground white pepper**

Put the Parmesan and 750ml cold water into a saucepan. Place over a medium
heat and stir with a wooden spoon until the cheese has melted; do not let it boil.

Strain the Parmesan water through a muslin-lined sieve and season to taste with
white pepper.

mushroom and horseradish nage

serves 6

250g button mushrooms, thinly sliced
50g shallots, chopped
2 thyme sprigs
250ml court bouillon (see below)
50ml crème fraîche or double cream
4 tbsp grated horseradish (preferably fresh)
150g butter, cut into small cubes
salt and freshly ground pepper

Put the mushrooms, shallots, thyme and court bouillon into a saucepan and bring
to the boil over a medium heat. Reduce by half, then add the crème fraîche and
bubble for 5 minutes. Take the pan off the heat, add the horseradish, then whisk in
the butter a piece at a time. Pass the nage through a fine-meshed conical sieve,
season and serve.

court bouillon I make this in the same way as my vegetable
stock (page 33), adding 3 tbsp white wine vinegar along with the other
ingredients. It is most often used as a light aromatic poaching stock for
fish and shellfish, the vinegar adding an appropriate hint of acidity.
It also forms the base for the above nage.

This nage is the perfect complement to grilled or
barbecued lamb, beef and venison. It brings out all the flavour,
especially when the meat is cooked and served rare.

parsley nage with lemon grass

serves 6

100g flat-leaf parsley, stalks and leaves
   coarsely chopped
30g shallot, chopped
1 lemon grass stalk, split lengthways
300ml fish stock (page 30) or vegetable
   stock (page 33)
4 tbsp double cream
juice of ½ lemon
200g butter, chilled and diced
salt and freshly ground pepper
2 tbsp finely snipped parsley leaves

Put the chopped parsley, shallot, lemon grass and stock into a saucepan and cook very gently for 10 minutes. Remove the lemon grass, transfer the contents of the pan to a blender and whiz for 1 minute.

Pass the purée through a fine-meshed conical sieve into a clean saucepan, add the cream and lemon juice and bring to the boil. Bubble until the sauce is just thick enough to coat the back of a spoon very lightly.

Reduce the heat to as low as possible and incorporate the butter, a little at a time, whisking continuously. Season the sauce to taste with salt and pepper, stir in the finely snipped parsley and serve at once.

This light, fresh sauce has a gentle lemony flavour underlying the enticing aroma of parsley. Serve it with any poached or pan-fried fish, or with scallops and langoustines.

serves 8

350g very ripe tomatoes, peeled, deseeded
  and chopped
50g shallots, finely sliced
50g button mushrooms, finely sliced
1 thyme sprig
1 bay leaf
250ml vegetable stock (page 33)
pinch of sugar
50ml double cream
250g butter
salt and freshly ground pepper

Put the tomatoes, shallots, mushrooms, herbs, stock and sugar into a saucepan
and bring to the boil over a medium heat.

As soon as the mixture starts to bubble, lower the heat and reduce the liquid
by two-thirds. Now add the cream and let the sauce bubble for 3 minutes.

Off the heat, whisk in the butter, a little at a time. Strain the sauce through a
fine-meshed conical sieve into a clean saucepan and season with salt and pepper
to taste. The nage is now ready to use.

This nage is perfect with lightly poached crustaceans, or grilled
fish such as salmon escalopes or sole fillets. It can be enhanced
with a little snipped basil added at the last moment. If fresh
tomatoes are slightly lacking in flavour, add 1 tsp tomato purée.

White sauces offer a palette of soft, muted colours, from ivory through tones of cream, venturing towards the pale golden beige akin to freshly picked hazelnuts. The main components of these sauces are chicken stock or milk, often with added cream. These sauces are among my favourites, especially in autumn and winter, when their velvety smoothness adds a welcome comforting aspect to dishes. Béchamel is the undisputed queen of white sauces, the matriarch of so many other sauces, all well worth discovering. These sauces are almost always bound and thickened with a white or blonde roux, or egg yolks, and small pieces of butter may be whisked in at the end of cooking to smooth and bind the sauce. Depending on how the sauce will be used, I like to add flavourings, such as aromatic herbs, spices, sherry, horseradish or mustard. Poached poultry, white meat and fish are always enhanced when served with a white sauce.

white sauces

béchamel sauce

serves 4

This sauce features in a variety of dishes, including macaroni cheese (made with a touch of cream and grated Gruyère or Emmenthal), cauliflower cheese,

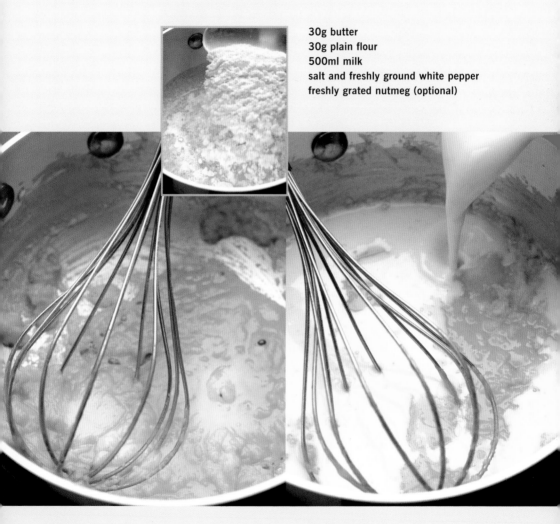

30g butter
30g plain flour
500ml milk
salt and freshly ground white pepper
freshly grated nutmeg (optional)

Melt the butter in a small, heavy-based saucepan over a low heat, then add the flour. Stir with a whisk, and cook gently for 2–3 minutes to make a white roux.

Pour the cold milk on to the roux, whisking as you do so, and bring to the boil over a medium heat, whisking continuously.

and a genuine croque monsieur. Béchamel also goes well with other vegetables, white meats, poultry and ham, and it forms the basis of many other sauces.

You can serve the sauce immediately or keep it warm in a bain-marie, in which case dot a few flakes of butter over the surface to stop a skin from forming.

When the sauce comes to the boil, lower the heat and simmer gently for about 10 minutes, stirring frequently. Season to taste with salt, white pepper and a little nutmeg if you wish, then the sauce pass through a fine-meshed conical sieve.

Béchamel sauce will keep in an airtight container in the fridge for up to 4 days. Reheat in a bain-marie.

soubise sauce Melt 40g butter in a saucepan over a low heat, add 200g thinly sliced onions and sweat for 5 minutes without colouring. Add 1 quantity of béchamel sauce, bring to the boil over a low heat and let bubble gently for 10 minutes, stirring frequently. Pass the sauce through a fine-meshed sieve into a clean saucepan, pressing the onions with the back of a small ladle to extract as much flavour as possible. Add 150ml double cream and cook gently for 6–8 minutes, stirring continuously, until the sauce has reduced and thickened. Season to taste with salt, pepper and nutmeg. This sauce goes particularly well with roast chicken or guinea fowl, or roast rack or loin of veal. Serves 4

aurora sauce Combine 300ml béchamel sauce and 100ml double cream in a saucepan and bring to the boil over a low heat, stirring with a whisk. Let the sauce bubble for 5 minutes, then add 100–120ml cooked tomato coulis (page 163) depending on its intensity. Bring back to the boil and cook for another 5 minutes, whisking continuously. Turn off the heat and whisk in 20g diced, chilled butter, a little at a time. Season the sauce with salt, pepper and/or nutmeg to taste. Pass through a fine-meshed conical sieve and serve. Hard-boiled eggs – sliced into discs, coated with aurora sauce and browned under the grill – are delicious. The sauce is also very good with poached eggs, pasta, cauliflower or grilled turkey escalopes. Serves 6

serves 4

20g butter
20g plain flour
150ml milk
350ml ham stock (see below) or
    chicken stock (page 28), cooled
2 tbsp chopped parsley
pinch of freshly grated nutmeg
salt and freshly ground white pepper

Melt the butter in a small, heavy-based saucepan over a low heat, then add the flour. Stir with a whisk, and cook gently for 2–3 minutes to make a white roux.

Pour the cold milk on to the roux, whisking as you do so, then whisk in the stock. Bring to the boil over a medium heat, whisking continuously as the sauce begins to bubble.

Add the parsley and simmer the sauce for 15 minutes, skimming the surface with a spoon if necessary. Season with the nutmeg and salt and white pepper to taste, then serve piping hot.

This sauce is especially good when made with the cooking liquid from a boiled ham and served with the ham. It also goes well with Brussels sprouts, carrots or potatoes. You can enrich the sauce with cream or butter, but I prefer it without.

mornay sauce

serves 4–6

30g butter
30g plain flour
500ml milk
pinch of freshly grated nutmeg
salt and freshly ground white pepper
3 egg yolks
50ml double cream
100g Gruyère, Emmenthal or Cheddar,
    finely grated

First make a béchamel. Melt the butter in a small, heavy-based saucepan over a low heat, then add the flour, stir with a whisk, and cook gently for 2–3 minutes to make a white roux.

Pour the cold milk on to the roux, whisking as you do so, and bring to the boil over a medium heat, whisking continuously. When the sauce comes to the boil, lower the heat and simmer gently for about 10 minutes, stirring frequently. Season to taste with nutmeg, salt and white pepper.

Mix the egg yolks and cream together in a bowl, then pour the mixture into the béchamel, whisking all the time. Let the sauce bubble for about 1 minute, whisking continuously, then take the pan off the heat and shower in the grated cheese. Stir until melted, then taste and adjust the seasoning if necessary.

You can coat poached eggs, fish, vegetables, white meats and many other dishes with this sauce, then lightly brown them under a hot grill. Or mix with macaroni to make a classic macaroni cheese.

coconut and chilli pepper sauce

serves 4

Serve this unusual, spicy sauce with firm-fleshed white fish,
such as brochettes of monkfish, or wide noodles.

30g butter
30g plain flour
400ml tinned coconut milk
freshly grated nutmeg
salt and freshly ground pepper
1 tbsp soy sauce
2 garlic cloves, crushed or finely chopped

for the chillies
100g butter
10g small hot red chillies, deseeded and
  finely chopped
20g hot green Jalapeño peppers, deseeded
  and finely chopped
250g small peeled shrimps or prawns (optional)

First make a coconut béchamel. In a small saucepan, melt the 30g butter and stir in the flour to make a roux. Cook over a low heat for 2 minutes, stirring all the time with a whisk.

Add the coconut milk, bring to the boil, then immediately season with nutmeg, salt and pepper and cook gently for 20 minutes, stirring continuously. Off the heat, stir in the soy sauce and garlic.

In another small saucepan, heat the 100g butter until it turns fragrant and golden brown. Toss in the chopped chillies and immediately tip the mixture into the coconut béchamel and stir until well amalgamated.

Adjust the seasoning if necessary and stir in the shrimps at the last moment, if you are using them. Serve hot.

illustrated on previous page

serves 4

20g butter
60g onions, chopped
400ml milk
1 whole or ½ onion (about 60g), studded
  with 2 cloves
80g white bread, crusts removed, cut into cubes
50ml double cream
salt and freshly ground white pepper

Melt the butter in a small saucepan, add the chopped onions and sweat gently for 1 minute. Pour in the milk, add the clove-studded onion and bring to a bare simmer. Cook gently, stirring occasionally, for 20 minutes.

Stir in the bread cubes and bring to the boil. Lower the heat and cook the sauce gently for 30 minutes, stirring occasionally with a wooden spoon.

Remove the studded onion, add the cream and let the sauce bubble gently for 5 minutes, whisking delicately. Season with salt and white pepper to taste and serve.

The perfect traditional sauce to accompany roast chicken, turkey, pheasant or grouse. Flavour with a little freshly grated nutmeg if you like.

velouté sauce

This velvety sauce can be served as it is, or used as the base for sauce suprême (see overleaf). Perfect with fish and chicken dishes, choose the stock accordingly.

30g butter
30g plain flour, sifted
1 litre cold fish stock (page 30), chicken stock
   (page 28) or vegetable stock (page 33)
salt and freshly ground pepper

First make a white roux. Melt the butter in a heavy-based saucepan. Off the heat, add the flour and stir it in with a whisk. Return to a medium heat and cook for 3 minutes, stirring continuously.

Pour the cold stock on to the roux, stirring all the time, then cook the sauce over a low heat for about 30 minutes, stirring occasionally with a whisk. Season with salt and pepper to taste.

albufera sauce Whisk 150ml veal demi-glace (page 27) into 500ml boiling chicken velouté, along with 50ml fresh or preserved truffle juice if you like. Season the sauce with salt and cayenne to taste and serve immediately. This wonderful rich sauce is ideal to accompany poultry, sweetbreads or calf's tongue. Serves 6

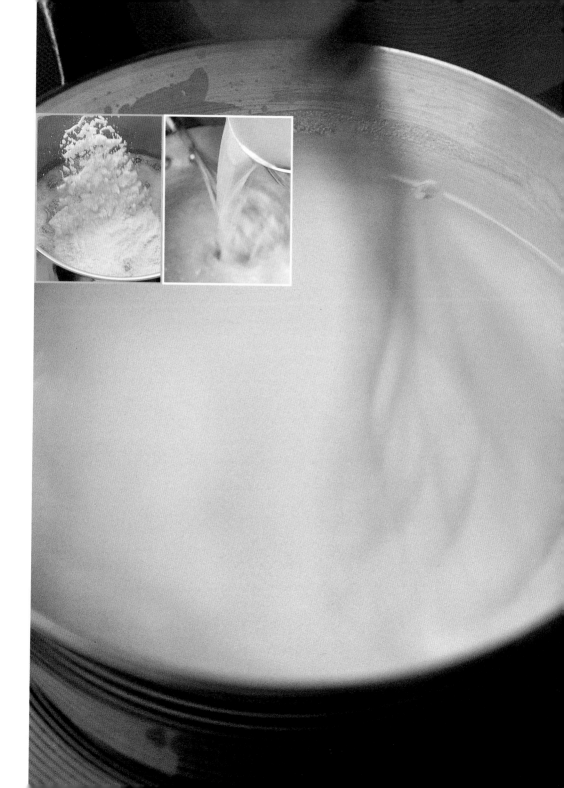

saffron sauce suprême

serves 4–6

This velvety sauce, prepared with a fish velouté, adds succulence to seafood and can be used as a filling for seafood crêpes. Made with chicken velouté, it is perfect with poached chicken, guinea fowl and poussin.

250ml fish or chicken velouté (page 66)
300ml double cream
½ tsp Dijon mustard
3g saffron threads
30g butter, chilled and diced
salt and freshly ground pepper

In a saucepan, heat the velouté, stirring occasionally with a whisk. As soon as it comes to the boil, add the cream and mustard and simmer gently for 5 minutes.

Put the saffron threads in the palm of one hand and rub them with the index finger of the other hand for 20 seconds, then add them to the sauce. Simmer for a further 5 minutes to allow the saffron to impart all its colour and flavour to the sauce, then pass it through a conical sieve into another saucepan.

Over a low heat, whisk in the butter, a piece at a time, then season the sauce with salt and pepper to taste. Serve at once.

minted sauce suprême Use a chicken velouté base. Replace the saffron with 30g finely snipped mint leaves, adding them to the sauce after you have strained it. I often serve this with roast rack or shoulder of lamb, or with sweetbreads.

sauce suprême with sherry and mushrooms

serves 4

250ml chicken velouté (page 66)
50g button mushrooms, thinly sliced
50ml double cream
30g butter, chilled and diced
4 tbsp dry sherry
salt and freshly ground pepper

Bring the chicken velouté to the boil in a saucepan and add the mushrooms and cream. Simmer over a low heat for 10 minutes, stirring occasionally with a wooden spoon.

Pass the sauce through a fine-meshed conical sieve into a clean saucepan, turn the heat to low and whisk in the butter, a little at a time.

Turn off the heat, stir in the sherry, season the sauce to taste with salt and pepper and serve immediately.

This smooth, creamy sauce has a subtle flavour and is the perfect match for poached poultry, veal escalopes, sweetbreads, braised lettuce and mushroom timbales.

This decadent sauce is perfect for a special occasion.
I like to serve it with veal chops or medallions.

75g fresh morels, or 30g dried morels
soaked in hot water for 30 minutes
400ml chicken velouté (page 66)
200ml Champagne
200ml double cream
80g foie gras butter (page 128)
salt and freshly ground white pepper

First clean the fresh morels. Trim the very bottom of the stalks, halve the mushrooms (or quarter them if they are very large), rinse in cold water to remove all traces of grit and delicately pat dry on a tea-towel. If using dried morels, drain them of their soaking water and proceed as for fresh morels.

Combine the chicken velouté and three-quarters of the Champagne in a saucepan. Bring to the boil and let bubble to reduce over a medium heat for 20 minutes.

Put the cream and prepared morels in another saucepan and bring to the boil over a medium heat. Cook for 5 minutes, then tip the cream and morel mixture into the velouté mixture. Cook at a bare simmer for 15 minutes, removing any skin from the surface with a spoon if necessary.

Add the remaining Champagne, let the sauce bubble for 2 minutes, then turn off the heat. Add the foie gras butter a little at a time, mixing it into the sauce with a wooden spoon. Season with salt and white pepper to taste and serve immediately.

mustard and white wine sauce

serves 4

This versatile sauce goes well with poached or braised
firm-fleshed fish, as well as pot-roasted poultry and other white meats.
Obviously you need to choose the stock you use accordingly.

30g butter
80g button mushrooms, thinly sliced
60g shallots, finely chopped
pinch of curry powder
1 tbsp Cognac or Armagnac
200ml dry white wine
1 small bouquet garni

200ml fish stock (page 30) or chicken
   stock (page 28)
300ml double cream
1 tsp English mustard powder, blended
   with 1 tbsp water
salt and freshly ground pepper
2 tbsp wholegrain mustard

Melt the butter in a saucepan, add the mushrooms and shallots and sweat for
1 minute. Stir in the curry powder and Cognac, then pour in the white wine. Bring
to the boil, add the bouquet garni and let bubble to reduce the liquid by one-third.

Pour in the stock, allow to bubble for 5 minutes, then add the cream and English
mustard. Cook until the sauce is thick enough to coat the back of a spoon.

Remove the bouquet garni, season the sauce to taste with salt and pepper and
pass through a fine-meshed conical strainer. Stir in the wholegrain mustard.
The sauce is now ready to serve.

allemande sauce

serves 6

60g shallots, finely chopped
100ml dry white wine
10 white peppercorns, crushed
1 bouquet garni, including a savory sprig
500ml chicken stock (page 28)
100g button mushrooms, sliced
200ml double cream
salt and freshly ground white pepper

for the liaison
100ml whipping cream
3 egg yolks
juice of 1 lemon

Combine the shallots, white wine, crushed peppercorns and bouquet garni in a saucepan. Bring to the boil over a medium heat and bubble to reduce the wine by two-thirds.

Add the chicken stock and mushrooms and cook until the liquid has reduced by half. Pour in the cream and let the sauce bubble for 5 minutes, or until it is thick enough to lightly coat the back of a spoon.

Meanwhile, for the liaison, lightly whip the cream to soft peaks, then fold in the egg yolks and lemon juice.

Pour the liason mixture into the sauce, whisking to combine. Immediately turn off the heat, season the sauce with salt and white pepper to taste and pass it through a fine-meshed conical sieve. Serve at once.

This light, silky sauce with its satisfying texture goes very well with poached poultry, sweetbreads and spinach ravioli.

300ml chicken stock (page 28), or
  broth from a pot-au-feu
150g horseradish, freshly grated, or
  200g bottled horseradish, well drained
300ml double cream
50g fresh white bread, crusts removed,
  cut into small cubes
1 egg yolk
1 tsp English mustard powder, blended
  with 1 tbsp water
salt and freshly ground white pepper

Combine the chicken stock or broth and the horseradish in a small saucepan set over a medium heat and boil until reduced by one-third. Add the cream and let bubble gently until reduced enough to thinly coat the back of a wooden spoon.

Transfer the sauce to a blender and whiz for 1 minute (you may have to do this in two batches), then pass through a fine-meshed conical sieve into a clean saucepan.

Add the bread cubes and cook over a low heat for 10 minutes, whisking all the time.

Turn off the heat, add the egg yolk and mustard and stir for a few moments to combine, then vigorously whisk the sauce to make it very smooth; it should have the consistency of porridge.

Season to taste with salt and white pepper and serve at once. If you need to keep the sauce warm, do so over a bain-marie; do not let it boil.

A legendary Roux brothers' sauce, this is particularly good
served with rabbit, pot-au-feu, silverside, veal knuckle and beef flank.

serves 6

With its hint of acidity and freshness, this sauce is ideal for serving with fish cakes or pan-fried lamb chops.

60g sorrel
30g butter
40g shallot, finely chopped
100ml white wine
200ml vegetable stock (page 33)
200ml double cream
salt and freshly ground pepper

Wash the sorrel and remove the stalks. Pile up several leaves, roll them up like a cigar and shred them finely. Repeat until you have shredded all the sorrel.

Melt the butter in a deep frying pan, add the shallot and sweat over a low heat for 30 seconds, then tip in the sorrel and sweat gently for another minute.

Pour in the white wine and vegetable stock and reduce the liquid by two-thirds. Add the cream and bubble for 2 minutes. The sauce should be thick enough to coat the back of a spoon lightly. Season with salt and pepper to taste and serve immediately.

A few shredded mint leaves added to the sauce just before serving intensifies the taste of the sorrel and gives the sauce a more rounded flavour.

caper sauce with anchovies

serves 8

500ml chicken velouté (page 66)
1 bouquet garni, including 1 or 2 savory
  sprigs if possible
100ml dry white wine
100ml double cream

60g anchovy butter (page 126)
salt and cayenne pepper
30g small capers (chop them if they
  are large), well drained
2 anchovy fillets, finely diced

Bring the chicken velouté to the boil in a saucepan, add the bouquet garni and white wine and cook gently for 10 minutes.

Pour in the cream and continue to cook gently for another 5 minutes. The sauce should lightly coat the back of a spoon; if it is not thick enough, increase the heat and reduce it for a few more minutes.

Lower the heat to minimum and whisk in the anchovy butter, a little at a time. Pass the sauce through a fine-meshed conical sieve into a clean saucepan and warm through gently. Season with cayenne and stir in the capers and diced anchovies. Taste and add a very little salt, if needed. Serve at once.

A lively, vigorous sauce that goes well with poached cod or brill. It will also cut the richness of offal, such as sweetbreads and tripe.

This is excellent with braised fish steaks, such as turbot or brill – adding a spoonful of the braising liquid to the sauce will enhance the flavour.

60g shallots, very finely sliced
1 small bouquet garni
4 juniper berries, crushed
300ml mild light beer
200ml double cream
60g butter, chilled and diced
2 tsp finely snipped flat-leaf parsley
salt and freshly ground pepper

Put the shallots, bouquet garni and juniper berries in a saucepan, pour in the beer and bring to the boil. Let bubble over a medium heat to reduce by two-thirds.

Add the cream and bubble for 5 minutes until the sauce is thick enough to lightly coat the back of a spoon. If it seems too thin, cook it for a few more minutes.

Pass the sauce through a fine-meshed conical sieve, whisk in the butter, a little at a time, and finally stir in the parsley. Season to taste with salt and pepper.

These sauces are refined and unctuous, yet delicate and so tempting that you want to eat them from a spoon. My particular favourite is hollandaise – served warm with steamed, poached or lightly grilled fish or with asparagus, it is sublime. It also forms the basis for béarnaise and many other delectable variations. Similarly, numerous cold emulsion sauces derive from classic mayonnaise, which can be lightened with whipped cream, yoghurt or fromage frais. The famous beurre blanc sauces are also included, at the end of the chapter. Always use a top quality white wine or Champagne without too much acidity for these. If you are serving a beurre blanc with braised white fish (turbot, for instance), you can substitute sherry vinegar. Because warm emulsion sauces are so delicate, it is best to make them just a few moments before serving. They cannot be prepared ahead and reheated, or kept warm for more than 20 minutes in a bain-marie, or they will lose their wonderful light texture.

A final note: use only extremely fresh or pasteurised eggs, especially if serving these sauces to pregnant women, the elderly or young children.

emulsion sauces

mayonnaise

makes about 300ml

Mayonnaise has many uses and is especially good with fish and seafood.

2 egg yolks, at room temperature
1 tbsp strong Dijon mustard
salt and freshly ground pepper
250ml groundnut oil (or use one-third olive oil;
  two-thirds groundnut oil)
2 tbsp white wine vinegar or lemon juice

Stand a mixing bowl on a tea-towel on the work
surface. Put the egg yolks, mustard, a little salt and
pepper into the bowl and mix with a balloon whisk.

Slowly add the oil in a thin trickle to begin with,
whisking continuously.

For a lighter mayonnaise, fold in 50–100g plain yoghurt or fromage frais, or 2 tbsp crème fraîche or whipped double cream at the end. Classic mayonnaise is also the basis for various other sauces (see overleaf). It can be kept covered for several hours in a cold place.

..ayonnaise begins to thicken, add the oil ιeady stream, still whisking all the time.

When the oil is completely incorporated, whisk more rapidly for 30 seconds until the mayonnaise is thick and glossy. Add the vinegar or lemon juice, taste and adjust the seasoning as necessary.

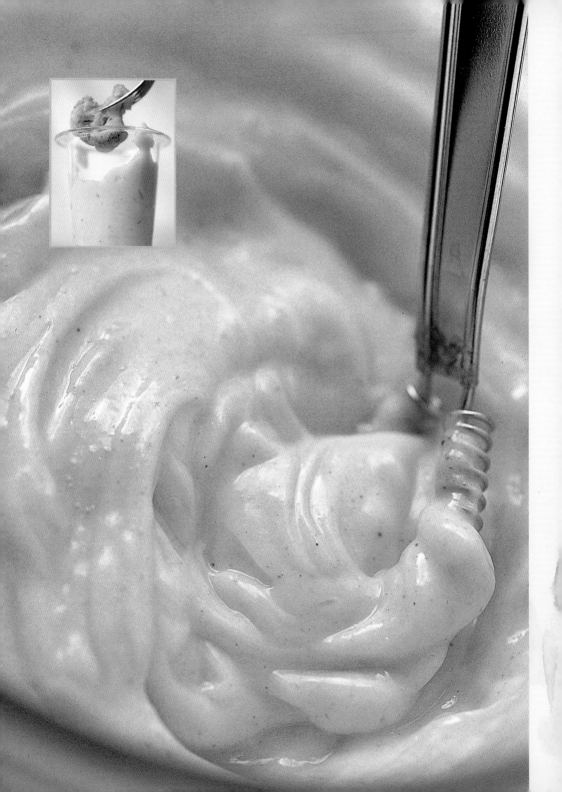

curry mayonnaise Dissolve 1 tbsp curry powder (mild or hot, to taste) in the lemon juice or vinegar before stirring it into the mayonnaise. Check the seasoning and whisk for another 30 seconds. This mayonnaise goes well with crudités, vegetable tempura, hard-boiled eggs, cold roast chicken and any cold poached firm-fleshed white fish. Serves 4–6

tomato mayonnaise Flavour the finished mayonnaise with 2 or 3 tbsp reduced cooked tomato coulis (page 163). Serves 4–6

bagnarotte sauce Flavour the mayonnaise with 3 tbsp tomato ketchup, 1/2 tsp Worcestershire sauce, 1 tbsp Cognac (optional), 2 tbsp double cream, 6 drops of Tabasco and the juice of 1/2 lemon. Whisk well to combine and season with salt and pepper to taste. Refrigerate until ready to use. This refreshing sauce is delicious with fresh crab, ripe tomatoes and cucumber, and with poached or hard-boiled eggs. Serves 6

alicante sauce Finely chop the blanched and refreshed zest of 1 orange and whisk into 1 quantity mayonnaise, made with 1 tbsp each lemon and orange juice (no vinegar). Season with paprika to taste. Beat 2 egg whites with a pinch of salt until stiff, then delicately fold into the mayonnaise. Serve immediately. Delicious with cold asparagus. Serves 6

rémoulade sauce Finely chop 40g cornichons or gherkins, 20g capers and 1 anchovy fillet and fold into the mayonnaise with 1 tsp Dijon mustard and 1 tbsp each snipped flat-leaf parsley, chervil and tarragon, using a spatula. Season to taste. This piquant sauce is perfect for a cold buffet, with assorted cold meats or as a condiment for picnic food like pressed tongue and cold roast chicken. Serves 6

sea urchin sauce Snip open 12 sea urchins with scissors, scrape out the corals and rub through a fine sieve, then fold into the mayonnaise. Whip 100ml whipping cream to a ribbon consistency and delicately fold into the mayonnaise with 1 tbsp Grand Marnier and 6 drops of Tabasco. Season with salt to taste. This delicate sauce accentuates the flavour of cold crustaceans such as lobster, crab, spider crab and langoustines. Serves 6

gribiche sauce

serves 6

This piquant sauce is especially good served with cold fish,
crustaceans, smoked trout and hard-boiled eggs.

4 hard-boiled eggs (freshly cooked)
1 tsp strong Dijon mustard
salt and freshly ground pepper
250ml groundnut oil
1 tbsp white wine vinegar
30g small capers, drained (chopped if large)
30g cornichons, finely diced
2 tbsp fines herbes (page 12), finely snipped

Separate the hard-boiled egg whites and yolks. Put the yolks, mustard and a little
salt and pepper into a mortar and crush with the pestle to make a smooth paste.

Gradually trickle in half of the groundnut oil, mixing with the pestle as you go
to amalgamate it thoroughly. Still mixing, add the wine vinegar, then continue
to trickle in the remaining oil as before.

Coarsely chop the hard-boiled egg whites. Add to the sauce with the capers,
cornichons and herbs and mix them in with a spoon. Season the sauce with salt
and pepper to taste.

180g baked potato pulp
2 hard-boiled eggs, yolks only
4 garlic cloves, crushed
1 raw egg yolk
salt and cayenne pepper
200ml olive oil
pinch of saffron threads, infused in
   3 tbsp boiling water

Rub the potato pulp, then the hard-boiled egg yolks through a sieve and put into a mortar with the garlic, raw egg yolk and a pinch of salt. Crush these ingredients together with a pestle until well amalgamated.

Now start to trickle in the olive oil in a thin, steady stream, working the mixture continuously with the pestle. When about half of the oil has been incorporated, add the saffron infusion, still mixing as you go.

Trickle in the remaining oil, working it in with the pestle to make a smooth, homogeneous sauce. Season with a good pinch of cayenne and salt to taste.

Aïoli is excellent with salt cod, bouillabaisse (better than the traditional rouille), fish soups and Mediterranean vegetables. Potatoes don't figure in the classic version, but I like the rustic, creamy quality they lend.

tartare sauce

serves 6

Tartare sauce is a classic accompaniment to fried and grilled fish; it is also served with cold fish and shellfish.

3 hard-boiled eggs, yolks only
salt and freshly ground pepper
200ml groundnut oil
1 tbsp wine vinegar or lemon juice
20g onion, finely chopped, blanched,
    refreshed and drained
3 tbsp mayonnaise (page 82)
1 tbsp snipped chives

Put the egg yolks into a mortar and pound with the pestle to make a smooth paste. Season with salt and pepper, then incorporate the groundnut oil in a thin stream, stirring continuously with the pestle.

When the oil is all incorporated, add the wine vinegar or lemon juice, then the onion and mayonnaise. Stir to combine, then add the chives and season with salt and pepper to taste.

This is a fresh, light and healthy sauce that goes extremely well with cold vegetables, fish, shellfish and poultry to be served as a starter or buffet.

1 hard-boiled egg, yolk only
1 raw egg yolk
1 tbsp strong Dijon mustard
300g natural yoghurt
generous pinch of wasabi powder or
    smoked paprika
juice of 1 lemon
fine sea salt

Press the hard-boiled egg yolk through a fine sieve into a large bowl. Add the raw egg yolk and then the mustard. Using a small whisk, work the ingredients together until evenly combined.

Stir in the yoghurt gradually as you whisk, as you would for a mayonnaise. Once the mixture is well combined, add the wasabi or paprika, the lemon juice and salt to taste. Transfer to a small bowl, cover with cling film and keep in the fridge until ready to serve, for up to 3 days.

When it's in season, I sometimes use freshly grated horseradish instead of wasabi.

honey mustard sauce

serves 6

40g runny honey (preferably mountain honey)
125g strong Dijon mustard
generous pinch of English mustard powder
½ tsp lemon juice

Put all the ingredients into a blender and process for 2–3 minutes until smooth and well combined.

I first came across this very mustardy sauce a few years ago in the Campton Place Hotel in San Francisco. I love it with squid or king prawn tempura, dipping each morsel lightly into the sauce as I eat them. Use an aromatic, perfumed honey for optimum flavour.

green sauce

This mayonnaise-based green sauce is wonderful served with cold fish, such as smoked trout or smoked eel. The chlorophyll can be used to add a unique herby flavour to many other hot or cold sauces.

1 quantity mayonnaise (page 82)
salt and freshly ground pepper

for the chlorophyll
200g leaf spinach, washed and stalks removed
10g chervil, washed and stalks removed
20g parsley, washed and stalks removed
10g tarragon, washed and stalks removed
10g chives
10g shallot, peeled and thinly sliced
trickle of groundnut oil (optional)

To make the chlorophyll, put the spinach, herbs, shallot and 350ml water into a blender and whiz at low speed for 1 minute. Increase the speed to medium and whiz for another 4 minutes.

Drape a piece of muslin loosely over a saucepan and secure it with an elastic band. Pour the herb purée on to the muslin and let it drip through slowly. After 10 minutes, gather up the edges of the muslin and squeeze to extract as much liquid as possible. Discard the herb residue and rinse the muslin in cold water.

Set the pan over a low heat and bring the liquid to a simmer, stirring occasionally with a wooden spoon. Add a pinch of salt and, when the liquid begins to tremble, turn off the heat. Stretch the muslin very loosely over a bowl and secure as before, then delicately ladle in the contents of the pan. Leave for about 20 minutes to drain.

Use a spatula to scrape the soft green purée (chlorophyll) from the surface of the muslin and place in a ramekin. (It will keep for several days in the fridge covered with a film of groundnut oil.)

To make the green sauce whisk a spoonful or two of the chlorophyll into the mayonnaise, to taste. Check the seasoning, then serve.

vincent sauce

Mix $^1/_2$ quantity green sauce and $^1/_2$ quantity tartare sauce (page 88) together, using a whisk. This sauce is perfect with cold poached salmon, hake or turbot. Serves 6

hollandaise sauce

serves 6

This light, creamy classic has inspired a host of other sauces.

1 tbsp white wine vinegar
1 tsp white peppercorns, crushed
4 egg yolks
250g butter, clarified (page 23)
   and cooled to tepid
salt
juice of ½ lemon

In a thick-bottomed stainless steel or copper saucepan, mix the wine vinegar with 4 tbsp cold water and the crushed peppercorns. Let bubble to reduce by one-third, then leave to cool completely. Add the egg yolks to the cold reduction and mix with a whisk.

Put the saucepan on a heat diffuser over a very low heat and continue whisking, making sure that the whisk comes into contact with the bottom of the pan.

Hollandaise cannot be kept waiting, so serve it as soon as it is made, or keep it covered for a short time in a warm place if you must.

Gradually increase the heat so that the sauce emulsifies progressively, becoming very smooth and creamy after 8–10 minutes. Do not allow the temperature of the sauce to rise above 65°C.

Off the heat and still whisking, pour in the tepid clarified butter in a steady stream. Season with salt to taste. At the last moment, stir in the lemon juice. Pass the sauce through a muslin-lined conical strainer to eliminate the crushed pepper if required, then serve immediately.

mustard hollandaise
Whip 75ml double cream to a ribbon consistency and mix in 30g Dijon mustard powder. Whisk the mustard cream into the hollandaise little by little. Season to taste and serve immediately. An excellent accompaniment to grilled salmon steaks, this sauce is also delicious with steamed courgettes. Serves 6

noisette sauce
Add 50g foaming browned butter to the finished hollandaise. This sauce is even more delicate than a hollandaise, and is particularly good with fish. Serves 8

mousseline sauce
Whip 75ml whipping cream to soft peaks and fold into the hollandaise just before serving. Adjust the seasoning. This subtle sauce is superb with poached or steamed fish, or with asparagus. When truffles are in season, I add some chopped truffle trimmings to make the sauce even more delectable. Serves 8

hollandaise with crustacean butter
Follow the recipe for hollandaise, reducing the clarified butter to 150g and gradually whisking 200g langoustine butter (page 132) or shrimp butter (page 131) in with it. Add 5g finely grated fresh root ginger with the lemon juice. Whip 50ml whipping cream with the juice of 1/2 lemon to a floppy consistency and fold into the sauce. Season with salt and pepper and serve immediately. This sauce is particularly good with grilled lobster or pan-fried cod garnished with langoustines. Serves 6

maltaise sauce
Zest 1 large or 2 small oranges (preferably blood oranges). Blanch the zest, refresh and chop very finely. Squeeze the juice and reduce in a small pan over a low heat by one-third, then add the zest and take the pan off the heat. Just before serving, whisk into the hollandaise together with the lemon juice. Season to taste and serve immediately. Delicious with poached salmon trout; also with asparagus and mangetout. Serves 6

hollandaise with mustard and horseradish
Mix 1 tbsp English mustard powder with 1 tbsp cold water and stir into the hollandaise along with 1 tbsp grated horseradish. Season to taste and serve. An excellent accompaniment to roast or grilled fish, this sauce is also delicious with steamed broccoli or with soft poached eggs. Serves 6

béarnaise sauce

serves 6

This sauce is equally good with grilled steak and beef fondue.
I also like to eat it on its own – spread on a piece of bread.

2 tbsp white wine vinegar
3 tbsp snipped tarragon
30g shallot, finely chopped
10 peppercorns, crushed
4 egg yolks
250g freshly clarified butter (page 23),
　　cooled to tepid
salt and freshly ground pepper
2 tbsp snipped chervil
juice of ½ lemon

Combine the wine vinegar, 2 tbsp snipped tarragon, the shallot and peppercorns in
a small, heavy-based saucepan and reduce by half over a low heat. Set aside to cool.

When the vinegar reduction is cold, add the egg yolks and 3 tbsp cold water. Set the
pan over a low heat and whisk continuously, making sure that the whisk reaches
right down into the bottom of the pan. As you whisk, gently increase the heat; the
sauce should emulsify slowly and gradually, becoming unctuous after 8–10 minutes.
Do not let it become hotter than 65°C.

Turn off the heat and whisk the clarified butter into the sauce, a little at a time.
Season with salt and pepper to taste and pass through a fine-meshed conical sieve
into another pan. Stir in the rest of the tarragon, the chervil and lemon juice. Check
the seasoning and serve.

choron sauce Add 2 tbsp well-reduced cooked tomato coulis (page 163)
to the finished béarnaise. Excellent served with fish en croûte.

paloise sauce Replace two-thirds of the tarragon with snipped mint.
Prepare as above, adding the tarragon and 1 tbsp mint at the start. Finish the sauce with
the chervil and remaining mint. Delicious with roast or grilled lamb.

rouille

serves 6

250g potatoes, peeled
1 garlic clove
3 hard-boiled egg yolks
250ml olive oil
salt and freshly ground white pepper
pinch of saffron threads

Boil or steam the potatoes until tender, then drain thoroughly and return to the pan. Toss over a medium heat for a few minutes to dry them out.

Peel the garlic clove and roll it in fine salt, then rub it round the inside of a bowl. Rub first the potatoes, then the hard-boiled egg yolks through a fine-meshed sieve into the bowl.

Stir with a spatula until well mixed, then gradually incorporate the olive oil, stirring continuously until very smooth. Season with salt and white pepper to taste and finally add the saffron.

Rouille is traditionally served with bouillabaisse, Mediterranean fish soups and mussel broths. Hand it round separately in a sauce boat so guests can help themselves. If you are a garlic lover, crush an extra clove and add it to the finished sauce.

This sauce is delicious with grilled fish, especially salmon, and vegetables such as cauliflower and broccoli. Chicken or fish stock can replace the vegetable stock if more appropriate to the dish.

200g red pepper
200ml vegetable stock (page 33)
1 small thyme sprig
4 egg yolks
60g butter, chilled and diced
salt and freshly ground pepper

Halve, core and deseed the red pepper, removing the pith. Chop the pepper coarsely and put into a small pan with the vegetable stock and thyme. Simmer for 15 minutes.

Tip the contents of the pan into a blender and whiz for 1 minute. Pass through a fine-meshed conical sieve into a small clean saucepan and leave until almost cold, then whisk in the egg yolks. Stand the pan in a bain-marie or on a heat diffuser over a very low heat and whisk the sabayon to a ribbon consistency.

Whisk in the butter, a little at a time, season the sabayon with salt and pepper to taste and serve at once.

beurre blanc with cream

serves 6

Like all beurres blancs, this must be made with the best quality unsalted butter. Simple and delicate, it is delicious with most poached fish.

75ml dry white wine
75ml white wine vinegar
60g shallots, finely chopped
50ml double cream
200g butter, chilled and diced
salt and freshly ground white pepper

Combine the white wine, wine vinegar and shallots in a small, heavy-based saucepan and reduce the liquid over a low heat by two-thirds. Add the cream and reduce again by one-third.

Over a low heat, whisk in the butter, a little at a time, or beat it in using a wooden spoon. It is vital to keep the sauce barely simmering at 90°C as you incorporate the butter; it must not boil. Season to taste with salt and pepper and serve immediately, or if necessary, keep warm in a bain-marie for a few minutes.

beurre rouge with cream
You can make a red version of this sauce by using red wine vinegar rather than white.

serves 6

This sauce is wonderful with poached chicken or guinea fowl, and equally good with whole braised fish, such as John Dory or baby turbot.

50ml Champagne vinegar
60g shallots, finely chopped
1 thyme sprig
100ml Champagne
60g button mushrooms, very finely diced
250g butter, chilled and diced
salt and freshly ground white pepper

Combine the Champagne vinegar, shallots and thyme in a small, heavy-based saucepan and reduce the liquid by half over a low heat. Add the Champagne and mushrooms and continue to cook gently until the liquid has again reduced by half. Remove the thyme.

Over a low heat, whisk in the butter, a little at a time, or beat it in with a wooden spoon. It is vital to keep the sauce barely simmering at 90°C; don't let it boil. Season to taste with salt and pepper and serve at once, or if necessary, keep the sauce warm in a bain-marie for a few minutes.

cider beurre blanc

serves 6

80ml cider vinegar
60g shallots, finely chopped
100ml sweet cider
50g dessert apple (preferably Cox's),
   peeled and finely grated
250g butter, chilled and diced
salt and freshly ground pepper

Put the cider vinegar and shallots into a small, heavy-based saucepan set over a low heat and reduce the liquid by half. Add the cider and grated apple and cook gently to reduce the liquid by one-third.

Still over a low heat, incorporate the butter, a little at a time, using a whisk or small wooden spoon. The butter sauce must not boil, but merely tremble at about 90°C. Season with salt and pepper to taste and serve immediately, or keep the sauce warm for a few minutes in a bain-marie.

This butter sauce is superb with grilled scallops, braised turbot, a simply poached sole on the bone, or an oven-roasted whole John Dory.

Vinaigrettes are always popular, but they really come into their own in summer – dressing delicate salad leaves, crudités of thinly sliced crisp baby vegetables, or a colourful *salade gourmande* of mangetout, mushrooms and seafood or fine slices of smoked fish. Some vinaigrettes will be transformed by the addition of a spoonful of vegetable purée, Américaine sauce or the pan juices from roast meat or chicken. Fresh herbs – especially chervil, tarragon and flat-leaf parsley – add a delicate, colourful note, so don't hesitate to use them. Vary the dressings to add interest to your salads. Oils and vinegars form the basis of all vinaigrettes (see page 109); just add your chosen flavourings – mustard, soy sauce, lemon, or a little yoghurt, fromage frais or crème fraîche. Flavoured butters with their palette of lovely colours are well worth making. Roll them into sausage shapes, wrap in greaseproof paper or cling film and firm them up in the fridge. Then slice off discs, allowing 30g per person, and pop them on to vegetables, meats and fish to enhance the flavour. I like to serve toasted croûtons topped with rosettes of shrimp or langoustine-flavoured butters as an aperitif.

vinaigrettes,
flavoured oils & butters

classic vinaigrette

This is the classic French vinaigrette. Everyone has his or her own take on this simple recipe, adding a pinch of sugar here, some garlic, chopped onion or raw egg yolk there… but all resulting in a dressing that cannot, in a traditional sense, be called a true vinaigrette.

1 tsp strong Dijon mustard
salt and freshly ground pepper
1 tbsp red or white wine vinegar
3 tbsp groundnut, sunflower or
   grapeseed oil

Put the mustard in a bowl with salt and pepper to taste. Whisk together, then pour in the vinegar as you whisk.

Finally, add the oil in a steady stream, whisking all the time. Taste and adjust the seasoning, and add a few more drops of vinegar if you feel it is needed.

Vinaigrette will keep for up to a week in the fridge, in a sealed jar or bottle.

vinegars Those most commonly used in vinaigrettes are red and white wine, sherry, balsamic and Champagne vinegars. I find industrially produced wine vinegar acidic and unexciting, and instead recommend using Orleans vinegar *(vinaigre d'Orléans)*, which is made and aged in oak barrels. It is full-bodied and crisp, and has a perfect balance of acidity with no hint of acridity. Cider vinegar and herb vinegars, including tarragon and rosemary, work well too. Fruit vinegars, like raspberry and blackcurrant, also make interesting vinaigrettes; these are best homemade.

oils The most popular oils are olive, groundnut, sunflower, corn, grapeseed, hazelnut, walnut and sesame. Some of these (nut and sesame oils, in particular) can be heavy, so it is preferable to lighten the taste by using a proportion of grapeseed or sunflower oil.

thai vinaigrette with lemon grass
In a bowl, combine a finely chopped 4cm piece of lemon grass, 15g finely shredded coriander leaves, 10g finely snipped chives, 2 tbsp Thai fish sauce, 1 tsp soy sauce, 200ml sunflower oil and 75ml rice wine vinegar. Whisk to combine and season with pepper to taste. Cover and leave to infuse for 2 hours before using. This refreshing vinaigrette is ideal for crisp leaves like Cos or batavia. It also makes an excellent dressing for rice noodles – the addition of some prawns, sesame seeds and extra coriander leaves makes it even more tempting. Serves 10

basil vinaigrette
Whiz 6 tbsp olive oil, 2 tbsp red wine vinegar, 15g snipped basil leaves, 1 finely chopped small garlic clove, 30g finely chopped shallot and 40g very ripe tomatoes in a blender for 30 seconds. Season with salt and pepper to taste. Use this vinaigrette with pasta, green beans and potato salads. Serves 6

lemon and mint vinaigrette
In a bowl, whisk the finely grated zest and juice of 2 lemons with 6 tbsp groundnut oil and salt and pepper to taste. Stir in 6 finely snipped mint leaves just before serving. This refreshing vinaigrette is perfect with watercress; it also makes an excellent dressing for grated carrots or a warm salad of cooked cauliflower. Serves 6

saffron vinaigrette
In a small saucepan, warm 3 tbsp white wine vinegar, add a generous pinch of saffron threads, turn off the heat and leave to infuse until cold. Whisk in 6 tbsp groundnut oil, 1 tbsp sesame oil, 1 tsp soy sauce, and salt and cayenne pepper to taste. A lovely dressing for a salad of tender leaves like lambs' lettuce and oak leaf, garnished with scallops or warm grilled langoustine tails and a few coriander leaves. Serves 6

tomato vinaigrette
Put 150ml tomato juice (ideally freshly pressed from very ripe tomatoes) in a bowl with 50ml olive oil, 50ml sherry vinegar, 5g snipped fresh basil or coriander leaves and some salt and cayenne pepper. Mix gently and check the seasoning, which should be quite assertive. Keep in the fridge until ready to use, but for no longer than 48 hours. A good dressing to enliven a fresh pasta or rice salad. Serves 6

cucumber vinaigrette
Peel 250g cucumber with a potato peeler, halve it lengthways, scoop out the seeds, then slice as thinly as possible, ideally using a mandolin. Place in a bowl and add 60g finely chopped shallot, 1 tsp each snipped chives, tarragon and flat-leaf parsley or chervil, 6 tbsp olive oil and 2 tbsp rice wine vinegar. Toss to combine, seasoning to taste with salt and pepper. Keep covered with cling film until needed. This fresh-tasting vinaigrette is lovely in summer with crisply cooked green beans or thinly sliced button mushrooms. Serves 4

roquefort vinaigrette
In a bowl, whisk together 3 tbsp walnut oil, 3 tbsp sunflower oil, 2 tbsp tarragon vinegar, 50g finely crumbled Roquefort, 1 tsp snipped tarragon leaves, a few drops of Worcestershire sauce and salt and pepper to taste. This dressing is particularly good with bitter winter leaves like dandelion, frisée and escarole, or crisply cooked warm French beans. Serves 6

parmesan vinaigrette
In a bowl, mix 1 tsp English mustard powder with 2 tbsp Champagne vinegar, then whisk in 6 tbsp double cream, 30g freshly grated Parmesan and 1 tbsp snipped chives. Season to taste and thin with a little warm water if necessary. This vinaigrette goes well with raw chicory, spinach or sliced mushrooms. Serves 6

truffle vinaigrette In a bowl, combine 6 tbsp olive oil, 2 tbsp red wine vinegar, 60g finely chopped black truffle, $1/2$ very finely chopped small garlic clove and 1 very finely chopped rinsed anchovy fillet, mixing with a spoon. Season to taste with salt and pepper and stir in 2 sieved or very finely chopped hard-boiled egg yolks just before serving. This vinaigrette is delightful with a salad of frisée or escarole, or with warm baby new potatoes, pasta or briefly cooked young, tender leeks. Serves 6

anchovy vinaigrette In a small pan, warm 3 tbsp olive oil to about 50°C, add 1 finely chopped garlic clove and infuse for 30 seconds. Add 75ml vegetable stock (page 33) and heat to 50–60°C. Turn off the heat, whisk in 3 finely chopped anchovy fillets, 6 finely chopped green olives, 2 tbsp balsamic vinegar and pepper to taste. Drizzle warm over pan-fried fillets of red mullet, bream or bass, or tender cooked artichokes. Serves 6

crustacean oil vinaigrette In a bowl, whisk 100ml crustacean oil (page 124) with 1 tbsp wholegrain mustard, the juice of 1 lemon and 1 tbsp snipped tarragon leaves. Season to taste with salt and pepper. Serve this dressing with freshly cooked noodles tossed with shellfish; it is also excellent with poached lobster. Serves 6

caesar dressing In a bowl, mix 1 egg yolk, $1/8$ tsp Dijon mustard, 1 tbsp lemon juice and $1/8$ crushed garlic clove with a small whisk until smooth. Add 1 tbsp anchovy essence, then slowly whisk in 75ml groundnut oil until amalgamated. Add 30g freshly grated Parmesan, and finally whisk in 2 tbsp water to give a slightly looser consistency. Season with pepper to taste. The classic dressing for a Caesar salad, this is well suited to robust salad leaves, such as Cos. Serves 6

low calorie vinaigrette In a bowl, whisk together 1 tsp wholegrain mustard and the juice of 2 lemons. Stir in 120ml tomato juice (preferably fresh), 25g finely chopped onion, 2 tbsp olive oil and salt and pepper to taste. Add 1 tbsp snipped basil or tarragon leaves just before serving. Serves 6

citrus vinaigrette

finely pared zest and juice of 1 orange
finely pared zest and juice of 1 lemon
1 tbsp caster sugar
1 tsp Dijon mustard
salt and freshly ground pepper
6 tbsp groundnut oil
1 tbsp finely chopped parsley

Cut the citrus zests into fine julienne. Blanch them separately in a pan of boiling water for 1 minute, then drain thoroughly.

Put the orange zest and juice into a small saucepan with the sugar and heat slowly to dissolve the sugar. Let bubble over a low heat until reduced by two-thirds, then remove from the heat and set aside.

In a bowl, whisk together the mustard, lemon juice and salt and pepper to taste. Whisk in the groundnut oil, then the reduced orange juice and zest. Just before serving, stir in the lemon zest and parsley.

This vinaigrette is good with all salads, particularly winter salad leaves such as escarole, chicory, frisée and radicchio.

serves 6

Cooked garlic is deliciously mellow and easy to digest.
This vinaigrette with its delicate aroma is perfect for well-flavoured
salads. Adjust the quantity of garlic to taste.

handful of coarse cooking salt
6 unpeeled fine plump garlic cloves
2 tbsp balsamic vinegar
salt and freshly ground pepper
3 tbsp groundnut oil
3 tbsp walnut oil
1 tbsp snipped chives

Preheat the oven to 180°C/Gas 4. Spread the coarse salt in a small roasting pan, arrange the garlic cloves on top and bake in the oven for 10 minutes. To check whether the garlic is cooked, insert the tip of a knife into the centre; it should meet with little resistance.

Remove the garlic cloves from the pan and use a fork to squash them out of their skins, one at a time, on to a plate.

Scrape the garlic purée into a bowl, add the balsamic vinegar and salt and pepper to taste and whisk until amalgamated, then whisk in the groundnut and walnut oils. Just before serving, stir in the chives.

flavoured vinegars

Vinegars flavoured with herbs and aromatics add interest to salad dressings. My suggested flavourings, and quantities for adding to 500ml full-bodied white or red wine vinegar, ideally Orleans vinegar *(vinaigre d'Orléans)*, are as follows:

shallot vinegar 100g baby shallots, peeled, blanched for 1 minute, then refreshed in cold water.

garlic vinegar 120g whole garlic cloves, peeled, blanched for 30 seconds, then refreshed in cold water.

rosemary vinegar 3 stems, blanched for 1 minute, then refreshed in cold water.

tarragon vinegar 40g tarragon sprigs, blanched for 30 seconds, then refreshed in cold water.

Pat your chosen flavouring ingredient thoroughly dry with kitchen paper, then place in a sterilised 500ml bottle. Pour in the vinegar through a funnel, leaving just enough room for the cork or stopper. Before placing in the bottle, immerse the cork (which should be brand new) in boiling water for 2 minutes, then refresh in cold water and pat dry. Alternatively, you can use a swing stopper bottle. Leave for at least 2 months before using, to allow the flavours to fully permeate the vinegar.

Note If you want to shorten the time between making and using the flavoured vinegar, you can bring the vinegar to the boil in a saucepan and, once it is tepid, pour it into the bottle over the flavouring. The flavoured vinegar will be ready to use much sooner, about 2 weeks after it is made. It will also keep longer, but has a little less vigour and freshness.

118

makes about 1 litre

Use to dress salads featuring shellfish, asparagus, artichokes and raw vegetables, and to deglaze the pan juices of fried or roasted red meats and game to lend an intensity to the sauce.

1.5kg very ripe raspberries, blackberries
  or blackcurrants
1.25 litres white wine vinegar
130g granulated sugar
200ml vodka or Cognac

Put half of the fruit into a non-metallic bowl and pour on the wine vinegar, making sure the fruit is submerged. Cover the bowl with a tea-towel or cling film and leave in a cool place for 24 hours. This is the first maceration.

Strain the first maceration of fruit through a fine-meshed sieve into a clean bowl, pressing very lightly with the back of a ladle to extract as much juice as possible without pushing through any pulp. Add the remaining fruit to the extracted juice, then cover and leave to macerate as before for 24 hours.

Strain the fruit through a fine-meshed sieve into a heatproof bowl or top of a double-boiler, pressing in the same way as before, then add the sugar and alcohol, and leave until the sugar has dissolved. Stand the bowl over a pan of hot water. Set over a high heat and bring to the boil. Lower the heat so that the water is just bubbling gently and cook the vinegar for 1 hour, skimming from time to time and topping up the bain-marie as necessary. The vinegar should remain at a constant 90°C throughout.

Pour the vinegar into a non-metallic bowl and leave in a cool place until cold. Strain through a muslin-lined conical strainer and a funnel into a sterilised bottle and cork it. The vinegar is now ready to use, and will keep for 3 weeks in the fridge.

NOTE If the fruit is not very sweet, increase the quantity of sugar by 10–15%. The precise amount of vinegar obtained will depend on how much juice the fruit contains (this can vary by up to 30%).

These are best made in small quantities (200–300ml at a time), as they will only keep for a few days – a week at the most – in the fridge. Once the bottle is opened, they quickly lose their aroma. It is essential to use very clean bottles with new, unused swing bottle stoppers, or bottles with a fairly wide neck that will fit a sterilised cork stopper. I choose flavoured oils for particular salads, and I also use them to brush meat or fish destined for the grill or barbecue. Adding a few spoonfuls to mayonnaise also works very well.

To make 200–300ml flavoured oil, use a light, fruity olive oil, or groundnut, sunflower or grapeseed oil, and choose from the following:

orange or lemon oil
Remove the zest of 3 oranges or lemons and dry out in a low oven at 110°C/Gas $^1/_4$ for 24 hours.

chilli oil
Use 3 dried jalapeño or serrano chillies. Add a few drops of chilli oil to pizza once it is cooked.

herb oil
Use 10g each of tarragon, chives and flat-leaf parsley, washed and well dried. If you are picking the herbs from your garden, do so first thing in the morning, before direct sunlight hits them, and never after it has rained.

garlic oil
Add 40g fresh, unblemished, unpeeled garlic cloves (they must be dry).

Heat your chosen oil in a saucepan until it registers 120°C (but no hotter) on a cooking thermometer (to destroy potentially harmful bacteria). Remove from the heat and add your chosen flavouring, then cover with the lid and leave to cool to room temperature.

Strain the oil through a fine-meshed conical sieve or muslin-lined funnel into small bottles, seal with sterilised corks or swing bottle stoppers and store in the fridge for up to 4 weeks until ready to use. Once opened, use within a week.

If you are making chilli or garlic oil, simply transfer the oil with the chillies and garlic to small bottles and keep the ingredients in the oil.

chive oil

makes 500ml

Drizzle this oil over grilled fish or add some to a vinaigrette to
impart a pronounced chive flavour.

500ml olive oil
50g chives, snipped

In a saucepan, heat the olive oil to about 80°C, then add the chives and cover the pan.
Immediately turn off the heat and leave the oil to cool.

Once cold, whiz in a blender for 30 seconds, then pass the oil through a fine-meshed
conical sieve, pour into a clean bottle and cork it. This flavoured oil will keep for
several days in a cool, dark place.

crustacean oil

124

makes about 1 litre

This delicately flavoured oil is one of my favourites.
It makes a superb dressing for seafood salads or warm asparagus.

1kg langoustines or crayfish, cooked
  in salted water
½ head of garlic (unpeeled)
1 thyme sprig
2 bay leaves

1 small bunch of tarragon
1 tsp whole white peppercorns
½ tsp whole coriander seeds
about 1 litre groundnut or olive oil
salt (for sterilising)

Preheat the oven to 120°C/Gas ½. Discard the eyes from the crustaceans and separate the heads, claws and tails. (Keep the tails to use as a garnish for fish or serve in a salad.) Roughly chop the heads and claws with a chef's knife, put them in a roasting pan and place in the oven to dry for 3 hours.

Put the dried crustacean heads and claws into a sterilised 1–1.5 litre kilner jar with the garlic, herbs, peppercorns and coriander seeds. Fill up the jar with oil to within 2 cm of the top and seal the lid carefully.

To sterilise the oil, you will need a saucepan at least as tall as the jar. Line the bottom and sides of the pan with foil; this will protect the glass, which might break if it should knock against the side of the pan. Stand the jar in the pan and pour in enough heavily salted water (300g salt per litre of water) to come up to the level of the oil, but not to submerge the jar. Bring the water to the boil over a high heat and boil for 35–45 minutes, depending on the size of the kilner jar.

After sterilisation, leave the jar at room temperature until completely cold, then refrigerate for at least 8 days before using the oil. It will keep for up to 4 weeks in the sealed jar in a cool place. Once opened, decant the oil into a bottle, store in the fridge and use within a week.

makes 500ml

500ml olive oil
50g mild fresh red chilli, finely chopped
1 thyme sprig
1 bay leaf
1 unpeeled garlic clove

In a saucepan, heat the olive oil to about 120°C. Add the chilli, herbs and garlic and cover the pan. Immediately turn off the heat and leave the oil to cool.

Once cold, pass through a fine-meshed conical sieve, then pour into a sterilised bottle and cork it. This flavoured oil will keep for up to 2 weeks in a cool, dark place. Once opened, use within a week.

Use this fragrant oil to add spiciness and zing to pizzas, pasta dishes and vinaigrettes.

maître d'hôtel butter

makes about 175g

This classic topping remains a favourite for grilled meat or fish.

150g butter, softened
20g parsley, chopped
juice of ½ lemon
salt
good pinch of cayenne pepper or
 freshly ground pepper

Put the softened butter into a bowl. Using a wooden spoon, work in the parsley, then mix in the lemon juice. Season to taste with salt and cayenne or black pepper.

Roll the butter into one or two sausage shapes in cling film, then wrap and refrigerate or freeze until needed.

horseradish butter Pound 50g grated fresh horseradish with a pestle and mortar, gradually adding 150g softened butter. Using a plastic scraper, rub through a drum sieve and season to taste. Shape, wrap and store as above. Serve with grilled white meats, or use to finish a sauce Albert (page 75), or pep up a béchamel (page 56). Makes about 200g

anchovy butter Whiz 50g chopped good-quality tinned anchovy fillets with 150g softened butter in a food processor. Season with pepper and a little salt if needed. Shape, wrap and store as above. Serve on grilled fish, or on toast canapés. Makes about 180g

caviar butter Mix 60g caviar (preferably pressed) into 150g softened butter, then, using a plastic scraper, rub it through a drum sieve. Season with salt and pepper to taste and use the same day. Superb on grilled fillets of sole or John Dory. Makes about 200g

pistachio butter Pound 100g skinned pistachio nuts to a paste with 1 tbsp water using a pestle and mortar, or whiz in a food processor. Mix in 150g softened butter and season with salt and pepper, then rub through a drum sieve using a plastic scraper. Using cling film, roll into one or two sausage shapes, wrap and refrigerate or freeze until ready to use. Delicious on grilled chicken, I also use this butter in my Sauternes sauce with pistachios (page 178), and sometimes add it to a hollandaise (page 94). Makes about 250g

roquefort butter Crumble 100g Roquefort and work into 150g softened butter with a wooden spoon. Whiz in a blender or rub through a drum sieve using a plastic scraper. Season with pepper to taste. Using cling film, roll the butter into one or two sausage shapes, wrap tightly and refrigerate or freeze until ready to use. Makes 250g

goat's cheese butter Cut up 150g fresh soft or semi-hard goat's cheese and pound using a pestle and mortar or whiz in a blender with 150g softened butter until evenly blended. Using a plastic scraper, rub through a drum sieve to eliminate any hard grains of cheese. Roll into one or two cylinders on a piece of cling film, wrap and refrigerate or freeze until needed. An appetising topping for grilled veal escalopes or chicken, this flavoured butter is also delicious tossed with pasta, along with a little snipped basil or parsley. Makes about 300g

foie gras butter Mix together 100g softened butter, 100g duck or goose foie gras and 2 tbsp Armagnac or Cognac with a wooden spoon, seasoning to taste with salt and pepper. Using a plastic scraper, rub through a drum sieve or whiz in a blender. Using cling film, roll into one or two sausage shapes and refrigerate or freeze until needed. Serve this delectable butter on toast canapés and grilled steak. Or use it to give a velvety finish to sauces, such as allemande (page 74), périgueux (page 210) and port (page 229). Makes about 200g

barbecue butter Put 150g softened butter into a bowl and mix in 1 tbsp chilli sauce, followed by 1 tbsp runny honey and 1 tbsp lemon juice, using a wooden spoon. Finally stir in 10g shredded mint leaves and season with salt and pepper to taste. Keep at room temperature until ready to use. Brush over barbecued meats just before serving. Makes about 175g

150g very fresh pink or brown shrimps
150g butter, softened
cayenne pepper (optional)

Rinse the shrimps in cold water, leaving any eggs attached. Drain and pat dry in a tea-towel.

Place the shrimps in a blender with the butter and a pinch of cayenne for extra zing if you like. Process for about 3 minutes, scraping down the sides a few times to ensure a homogeneous mixture. If you prefer, you can use a pestle and mortar instead of a blender.

Using a plastic scraper, rub the flavoured butter through a drum sieve to eliminate the shrimp shells. Using cling film, roll it into one or two sausage shapes and refrigerate or freeze until ready to use.

Sublime with pan-fried or grilled fish, this butter can also be used to enrich a fish sauce, or spread on toast croûtons to serve as canapés.

langoustine butter

makes about 450g

> I like to enrich fish sauces with this butter. It also makes wonderful canapés – spread on toast croûtons and topped with langoustine tails.

50g butter, preferably clarified (page 23)
1 small carrot, finely diced
1 medium onion, finely diced
12 crayfish or langoustines (preferably live)
5 tbsp Cognac or Armagnac
200ml white wine

1 small bouquet garni
2 pinches of cayenne pepper
salt and freshly ground pepper
about 250g softened butter (75% of the weight of the cooked crustacean heads and claws)

Melt the clarified butter in a deep frying pan. Add the carrot and onion and sweat until soft. Using a slotted spoon, transfer the vegetables to a ramekin, leaving the butter in the pan.

Add the crustaceans to the pan and sauté over a high heat for 2 minutes. Add the Cognac and ignite it. Once the flames have died down, pour in the white wine. Add the cooked vegetables, bouquet garni, a little cayenne and a small pinch of salt and cook gently over a low heat for 10 minutes. Tip the contents of the pan into a bowl and set aside to cool.

To make the flavoured butter, separate the crustacean heads and tails. Keep the tails for another use (canapés or a salad, perhaps). Gather up the heads and claws, and extract the creamy flesh from the heads. Weigh the mixture. Put into a food processor or blender with 75% of its weight of softened butter and the diced vegetables. Whiz until mushy.

Using a plastic scraper, rub the mixture through a drum sieve and season to taste with salt and pepper. Using cling film, roll the flavoured butter into one or two sausage shapes and refrigerate or freeze until needed.

makes about 200g

Spread this butter on toast canapés, serve with poached fish, or whisk into sauces, such as hollandaise (page 94), béchamel (page 56) or devil sauce (page 220) to enhance the flavour and colour.

170g butter, softened
60g red pepper, cored, deseeded and
    finely diced
1 thyme sprig
salt and freshly ground pepper

Melt 20g butter in a small saucepan and add the diced pepper and thyme. Sweat gently for 5 minutes, then set aside to cool. Discard the thyme.

Mix the cooled red pepper into the remaining softened butter with a wooden spoon and season with salt and pepper to taste. Using a plastic scraper, rub the mixture through a drum sieve, or whiz in a blender. Using cling film, roll the butter into one or two sausage shapes and refrigerate or freeze until ready to use.

paprika butter Melt 20g butter in a small saucepan, add 30g finely chopped onion and sweat gently for 2 minutes. Leave until cold, then mix into 150g softened butter. Add 1/2–1 tbsp paprika, and salt and pepper to taste. Whiz in a blender or rub the flavoured butter through a drum sieve using a plastic scraper. Using cling film, roll into one or two sausage shapes, wrap tightly and refrigerate or freeze until needed. Serve with grilled escalopes of veal, turkey or chicken. Makes about 180g

curry butter Prepare as for paprika butter, doubling the quantity of onion and the butter to sweat it in, and replacing the paprika with 1–2 tbsp curry powder, to taste. Add the curry powder to the onions after 1 minute, not directly to the softened butter. Good with grilled pork chops, chicken, turkey and veal. Makes about 180g

Salsas came originally from Mexico, but the Spanish and Indians, among others, have subsequently added their own touch of magic, ensuring that these fresh-tasting sauces are now familiar all over the world. They are vibrant in colour, easy to prepare, and stimulate and delight the taste buds. There are numerous different salsas, but the one thing they should all be is full of flavour, with a well-judged balance of herbs and spices. I like to serve a salsa, especially in summer, with ingredients whose flavours and colours work together harmoniously. The different flavourings intermingle and assert themselves best when the salsa is prepared several hours before being served. However, when avocado is included, this should be added just as the salsa is served, to prevent it from oxidising and turning black. Also included in this chapter is a selection of tempting piquant sauces to partner pasta dishes, soups, fish and white meat, not least my bois boudran sauce (on page 147), which I often serve with poached salmon and roast chicken.

salsas
& other piquant sauces

red pepper salsa serves 8

I like to serve this salsa with spaghetti or macaroni, but it is equally delicious eaten on toast or in bouchées as a canapé.

4 red peppers
2 small yellow peppers (optional)
2 shallots, finely chopped
2 small thyme sprigs, leaves only, chopped
10–12 basil leaves, snipped
salt and freshly ground pepper
125ml olive oil
juice of 2 lemons

Using your fingertips, oil the peppers very lightly. Grill them (ideally on a barbecue, otherwise under a very hot grill or in a hot oven) until the skins are blistered and blackened.

Plunge the charred peppers into a bowl of iced water to cool them quickly, then remove and peel off the skins. Halve the peppers, remove the core and scrape out the seeds and white membranes.

Serve the salsa immediately, or cover with cling film and keep in the fridge for up to 48 hours.

Cut the peppers into long, thin strips. If using yellow peppers, set them aside to add a final touch of colour to the salsa.

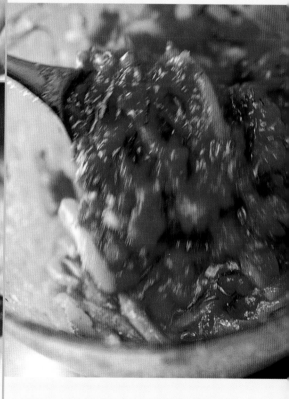

Dice the red peppers as finely as possible and place in a bowl. The texture should be almost pulpy – halfway between tiny dice and a coulis.

Add the shallots, thyme and basil to the red peppers, season with salt and pepper, and stir in the olive oil and lemon juice. Mix carefully, adding the yellow pepper julienne if using. Taste and adjust the seasoning if necessary.

herb salsa

serves 6

This salsa goes particularly well with pasta, especially tortellini or cappelletti filled with a mushroom stuffing. You can also serve it with steamed cauliflower or French beans as a starter, or with grilled tuna.

1 potato, about 60g
60g fines herbes (tarragon, chervil and
    flat-leaf parsley), snipped
40ml sherry vinegar
120ml olive oil

juice of 1 lemon
30g trimmed spring onions, finely
    chopped
1 tbsp coarse grain Meaux mustard
salt and freshly ground pepper

Boil the potato in its skin, then peel and press through the coarse blade of a vegetable mouli or potato ricer into a bowl.

Add all the other ingredients and stir to combine, seasoning with salt and pepper to taste.

green olive and lemon salsa Cook the potato and prepare as above. Combine in a bowl with 1 peeled and segmented lemon (all pith removed), the juice of 2 lemons, a pinch of saffron threads infused in 1 tbsp warm water, 12 finely diced green olives, 1 tbsp snipped flat-leaf parsley, 30g finely chopped spring onions and 100ml olive oil. Season with salt and pepper to taste. Serve as an accompaniment to salmon tartare, cold poached fish or vegetable crudités. Serves 6

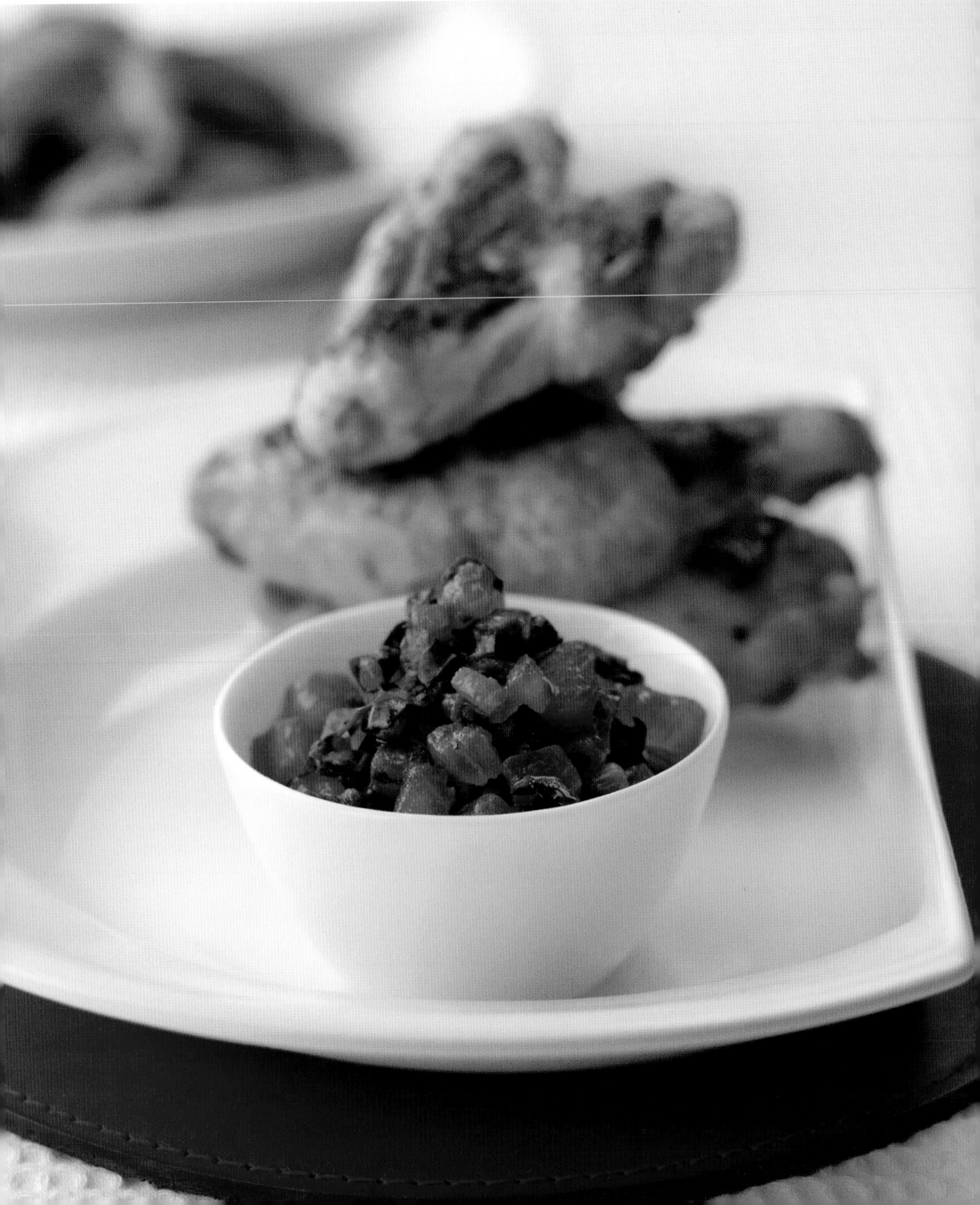

serves 6

A delicate salsa which goes beautifully with seafood, lightly cooked on the barbecue, and with fish. It also works well with cold chicken or veal.

200g very ripe tomatoes
3 tbsp rinsed, well-drained small capers
    in vinegar
50g black olives, pitted and finely diced
150ml olive oil
juice of 1 lemon
salt and coarsely ground white pepper
20g snipped basil leaves

Peel, deseed and dice the tomatoes and place in a large bowl. Add all the other ingredients, except the basil, seasoning with salt and white pepper to taste. Mix together with a spoon.

Cover with cling film and leave to stand for up to an hour to let the flavours mingle.

About 30 minutes before serving, add the basil and stir to combine. Serve the salsa at room temperature.

If you prefer a more rustic salsa, do not peel the tomatoes.

pineapple salsa with coriander

serves 4

A delicious salsa to go with barbecued dishes, such as pork spareribs or sausages, duck breast or swordfish. It is best served just warm, so should ideally be prepared at least an hour in advance.

1 tbsp soft brown sugar
300g peeled and cored fresh pineapple,
    cut into 1cm dice
½ red serrano chilli, finely diced
1 tbsp sambal oelek
1 tsp lime juice
2 tbsp chopped coriander leaves
small pinch of salt

Place a non-stick frying pan over a medium heat and sprinkle in the sugar. As soon as the sugar has melted and nearly caramelised, add the diced pineapple. Cook the pineapple, stirring every minute or so with a wooden spatula, until lightly caramelised, about 4–5 minutes.

Tip the pineapple into a large bowl and add the chilli, sambal oelek, lime juice and coriander. Mix well with a spoon, adding a touch of salt to taste.

Cover with cling film and set aside until ready to serve.

Not everyone is keen on fresh coriander. My advice when using it is to only include half the specified amount in the salsa, and serve the rest separately in a small dish. Alternatively, substitute half the quantity of coriander for chopped, flat-leaf parsley.

tropical salsa

serves 6

100g peeled and pitted fresh mango,
   cut into small dice
100g peeled and cored fresh pineapple,
   cut into small dice
1 very ripe kiwi fruit, peeled and cut
   into small dice

1 small onion, preferably red, about 60g,
   finely chopped
½ red serrano chilli, finely diced
1 tbsp chopped coriander leaves
1 tbsp lime juice
2 tbsp grapeseed or other mild-flavoured oil

Mix all the ingredients together very gently in a large bowl. Cover with cling film
and set aside for at least 2 hours before serving.

I recommend serving this salsa with small,
whole grilled fish, such as sea bass, bream or red mullet. As soon as the
fish is cooked, I remove the fillets from the bone, spoon the salsa over
them and serve 5–10 minutes later. It's simply delicious.

I serve this sauce with steamed fillets of red mullet and sea bass, and fresh pasta – especially cappelletti filled with lobster or other shellfish.

80g tomatoes
200ml olive oil
juice of 1 lemon
2 tbsp snipped basil leaves
1 tbsp snipped chervil leaves
1 garlic clove, finely chopped
6 coriander seeds, crushed
salt and freshly ground pepper

Peel, deseed and dice the tomatoes and place in a bowl with the olive oil, lemon juice, herbs, garlic and coriander seeds. Mix gently and season with salt and pepper to taste.

Just before serving, warm the sauce slightly, to about 30–40°C.

serves 6–8

300ml groundnut oil
50ml wine vinegar
salt and freshly ground pepper
150g tomato ketchup
1 tsp Worcestershire sauce
5 drops of Tabasco
100g shallots, chopped
5g chervil, finely snipped
5g chives, finely snipped
20g tarragon, finely snipped

Combine the groundnut oil and wine vinegar in a bowl. Add a pinch of salt and 3 turns of the pepper mill. Stir with a small whisk to emulsify.

Add the tomato ketchup, Worcestershire sauce, Tabasco, shallots and snipped herbs. Stir to combine, then taste and adjust the seasoning.

The sauce is ready to use right away, but it can also be kept in an airtight container in the fridge for up to 3 days. Return to room temperature before serving.

An excellent accompaniment to roast chicken or poussin, this lively sauce can also be used to coat a lightly poached fillet of salmon or trout just before serving.

yoghurt sauce

serves 6

This refreshing sauce is excellent with cold vegetables, fish and
hard-boiled eggs. It is very quick to make.

600ml natural yoghurt
100g mayonnaise (page 82)
2 tbsp snipped herbs of your choice
   (chervil, parsley, chives, tarragon, etc.)
1 medium marmande tomato
salt
small pinch of cayenne pepper, or
   4 drops of Tabasco

Mix the yoghurt and mayonnaise together in a bowl until evenly combined, then stir in the snipped herbs.

Peel, deseed and dice the tomato and fold into the sauce. Season with salt and cayenne pepper to taste. The sauce is now ready to serve.

The punchy, aromatic flavour of pistou enhances Mediterranean soups, pasta and steamed fish to delicious effect.

4 garlic cloves, halved
salt and freshly ground pepper
20 basil leaves
100g Parmesan, freshly grated
150ml olive oil

In a small mortar, crush the garlic to a purée with a pinch of salt (or use a small blender). Add the basil and crush to a homogeneous paste. Add the Parmesan.

Now trickle in the olive oil in a steady stream, stirring continuously with the pestle, as though you were making mayonnaise. Work the sauce until smooth. Season to taste with salt and pepper.

Use the pistou immediately, or transfer it to a bowl and cover with cling film. It will keep in the fridge for several days.

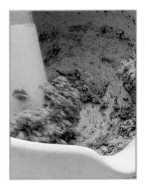

pesto Add 30g grilled or toasted pine nuts along with the basil for a classic Italian pesto, with its firmer, richer consistency. It is perfect stirred into a risotto or tossed with pasta just before serving, and has many other uses. Serves 6

ginger and chilli sauce for sashimi

serves 8

For sashimi, it is essential to use extremely fresh, good quality salmon and tuna. Cut into diamonds, about 5mm thick, arrange on a platter and serve with this sauce for a superlative result.

1 tbsp peeled fresh root ginger
2 tbsp fine julienne of spring onions
1 red serrano chilli, cut into very fine julienne
2 tbsp dark soy sauce
1 tbsp light soy sauce
1 tbsp unrefined cane sugar
2 tbsp chicken stock (page 28)
1 tbsp sesame oil
2 tbsp groundnut oil

Put all the ingredients, except the oils, into a large bowl. In a small pan, heat the oils to between 80 and 100°C (until a breadcrumb dropped into the pan just sizzles), then pour over the ingredients in the bowl, stirring with a fork.

Mix well, then cover the bowl with cling film and leave the sauce to stand for at least 20 minutes before serving.

As an optional extra, I sometimes serve coriander leaves and extra chilli julienne in a separate dish, for guests to help themselves.

Coulis sauces are light, smooth, full of flavour and glistening in colour… I sometimes catch myself eating them by the spoonful as I make them. They are also nutritious and, with the exception of cream-based coulis, very healthy. To lighten a vegetable coulis where cream is called for, you can omit the cream and add a small amount of crème fraîche or fromage frais (standard, not low fat) instead, to finish. If added towards the end of cooking, allow to boil for no more than a minute. Tomato and vegetable coulis go well with poached or grilled meats, and fish, and they are equally welcome in summer and winter. They should ideally be prepared only a short time before serving, to ensure they keep their intensity and vivid colour. If prepared a little in advance, reheating them in a bain-marie will help to preserve their velvety, smooth texture. My grandchildren often ask me to make a coulis for them, in particular a cep coulis, which they love mixing into pasta. I must admit that it is worth it… the pasta dish does take on a whole new dimension.

vegetable coulis

cucumber coulis

serves 6

This refreshing coulis goes well with cold poached fish, smoked salmon, cold omelettes and pasta salads.

1 medium cucumber
1 small red chilli, deseeded and diced
4–5 parsley sprigs, roughly chopped
6 sage leaves, roughly chopped
50ml olive oil
squeeze of lemon juice, to taste
salt and freshly ground pepper

Peel the cucumber, cut it in half lengthways and remove the seeds. Chop the cucumber into chunks and put into a blender.

Add the chilli to the blender (remembering to wash your hands afterwards). Whiz for 1 minute until the mixture is fairly smooth.

Pour the coulis into a bowl. Taste and adjust the seasoning, adding more lemon juice if needed. Cover and refrigerate until ready to serve.

Add the parsley and sage to the blender and process for another minute.

Now pour in the olive oil and add a generous squeeze of lemon juice. Blend for about 2 minutes until smooth and almost creamy.

This coulis will keep in the fridge for up to 48 hours, but the water in the cucumber will cause it to separate, so stir with a small whisk to combine just before serving.

asparagus coulis

This delicious sauce is almost as light as a nage.
I add some asparagus tips at the last moment and serve it with
delicate steamed fish or vegetable lasagne.

350g asparagus spears (preferably small)
salt and freshly ground pepper
50g butter
80g shallots, chopped
1 thyme sprig
300ml chicken stock (page 28) or water
300ml double cream
1 tsp soy sauce (optional)

Peel the asparagus stalks using a swivel vegetable peeler. Cut off the tips and
blanch them in boiling salted water for 1 minute or until firm to the bite.
Refresh, drain and set aside. Chop the stalks and leave them raw.

Melt the butter in a heavy-based saucepan. Add the chopped asparagus stalks
and shallots and sweat gently for 5 minutes. Add the thyme and chicken stock
and cook over a medium heat for 15 minutes.

Pour in the cream, increase the heat to high and reduce the coulis by one-third.
Whiz in a blender for 3 minutes, then pass through a fine-meshed conical sieve.
Season with salt and pepper to taste, adding the soy sauce if you wish.

Keep warm and serve as soon as possible. Add the blanched asparagus tips to
the coulis just before serving.

illustrated on page 153

serves 4–6

A chilled vegetable coulis makes an excellent accompaniment to cold poached fish.

360g celeriac, peeled and diced
salt and freshly ground pepper
300ml double cream

Cook the celeriac in a pan of boiling salted water until tender. Drain thoroughly and place in a blender.

Add 100ml cream and whiz to a very smooth purée. Transfer to a bowl and leave to cool, stirring from time to time.

Using a whisk, gently stir in the rest of the cream. Season the coulis with salt and pepper to taste and chill in the fridge until needed.

creamy carrot coulis Use carrots in place of celeriac.

creamy pea coulis Replace the celeriac with 500g shelled fresh peas.

leek coulis with saffron and dill

serves 6

This is one of my favourite coulis. It marries well with firm-fleshed fish like brill, monkfish and turbot, or seafood such as langoustine tails and scallops.

400g young leeks, white part only
50g butter
300ml chicken stock (page 28) or
   vegetable stock (page 33)

2 small pinches of saffron threads
300ml double cream
salt and freshly ground pepper
1 tbsp chopped dill

Halve the leeks lengthways, wash thoroughly in cold water and slice them finely. Blanch in boiling water for 2 minutes, then refresh in cold water and drain well, pressing the leeks to extract all moisture.

Melt the butter in a saucepan, add the leeks and sweat them gently for 10 minutes. Add the stock, then the saffron threads, and cook over a medium heat for barely 10 minutes. Add the cream and let bubble for 5 minutes.

Tip the mixture into a blender and whiz for 2 minutes. Strain through a fine-meshed conical sieve and season with salt and pepper to taste.

Keep the coulis warm if it is to be served soon; otherwise reheat it gently just before serving. Stir in the dill at the very last moment.

As with all savoury coulis, you can use vegetable rather than chicken stock to satisfy vegetarians.

aubergine coulis

serves 8

1 small aubergine, about 300g
1 medium tomato, about 100g
3 tbsp olive oil
60g chopped shallot
½ tsp finely chopped garlic
1 tsp thyme leaves
100ml chicken stock (page 28) or
   vegetable stock (page 33)
salt and freshly ground pepper
juice of 1 lemon

To prepare the aubergine, remove the stalk end, then wash in cold water and dry well. Just before cooking, chop the aubergine into small cubes. Peel, deseed and finely chop the tomato.

In a saucepan, gently heat the olive oil and add the shallot. Cook for 1 minute, then add the aubergine cubes. Increase the heat and cook, stirring every minute or so with a wooden spoon, until the aubergine softens a little.

Add the chopped tomato, garlic and thyme and cook for a further 5 minutes. Pour in the stock and cook over a gentle heat for 15 minutes.

Transfer to a blender and process for 5 minutes. Pass the coulis through a fine-meshed conical sieve and season with salt and pepper to taste. Add the lemon juice just before serving.

This lovely coulis is excellent with lamb chops, chicken breast fillets, or even grilled spatchcock quails. The smooth texture and fine aubergine flavour never fail to delight.

serves 4

750g very ripe marmande tomatoes
150ml olive oil
2 garlic cloves, crushed
60g shallots, finely chopped
1 small bouquet garni, with plenty
   of thyme sprigs
1 tbsp tomato concentrate (optional)
pinch of sugar
6 peppercorns, crushed
salt

First peel the tomatoes: cut a cross on the top and cut out the core, then immerse the tomatoes in a bowl of boiling hot water for 10–20 seconds until the skin starts to split. Take out and plunge into a bowl of iced water. Lift out with a draining spoon and slip off the skins.

In a heavy-based saucepan, warm the olive oil with the garlic, shallots and bouquet garni. After 2 minutes, add the tomatoes and tomato concentrate if needed (only if the fresh tomatoes are not fully ripe), along with the sugar and crushed pepper.

Cook very gently for about 1 hour, stirring occasionally with a wooden spoon until all the moisture has evaporated. Remove the bouquet garni.

Tip the contents of the pan into a blender and whiz to a smooth purée. Season with salt to taste.

The coulis is ready to use at once, or it may be kept in the fridge for up to 5 days. After reheating, add a little olive oil just before serving.

This coulis is particularly good with grilled fish. I also recommend adding a little to a fish sauce, or a béchamel for a pasta gratin.

fresh tomato and basil coulis

serves 6

350g very ripe tomatoes
1 tsp tomato concentrate (optional)
60ml sherry vinegar (preferably) or
    balsamic vinegar
8 coriander seeds, crushed
100ml olive oil
salt and freshly ground pepper
12 basil leaves, shredded

Whiz the tomatoes in a blender, then rub through a sieve into a bowl to give about 250ml purée. Add the tomato concentrate if needed (only if the fresh tomatoes are not fully ripe).

Add the sherry vinegar, coriander seeds and olive oil. Mix with a whisk until evenly combined and season to taste with salt and pepper. Finally, add the shredded basil.

The coulis is now ready to serve. Alternatively, it can be kept in a sealed container in the fridge for up to 3 days.

This vibrant, fresh-tasting coulis is especially good with a poached egg served on a bed of spinach. It is also an ideal partner for grilled chicken breasts or poached skate wings.

serves 6

This is excellent with poached or pan-fried poultry, or used as a dressing for pasta. Or, for a delicious starter, pan-fry ceps with a touch of garlic and parsley until crunchy, and serve them on a little cep coulis.

75g butter
30g shallot, chopped
300g fresh ceps, cleaned (or frozen ceps, thawed), finely sliced
300ml chicken stock (page 28)
1 small garlic clove, crushed
20g flat-leaf parsley, snipped
salt and freshly ground pepper

Melt 50g butter in a saucepan. Add the shallot, then the ceps and sweat over a low heat for 5 minutes. Add the chicken stock, garlic and parsley and cook over a medium heat for 10 minutes.

Tip the mixture into a blender and blend for 5 minutes until very smooth, then strain through a fine-meshed conical sieve.

Just before serving, dice the remaining 25g butter and reheat the coulis. Whisk in the butter, a piece at a time, season with salt and pepper to taste and serve.

serves 8

400g curly or flat-leaf parsley, stalks removed
salt and freshly ground pepper
300ml double cream
50g shallots, thinly sliced
100ml milk, heated to boiling

Wash the parsley in plenty of cold water. Bring a pan of lightly salted water to the boil and plunge in the parsley. Boil for 2 minutes, then refresh in iced water and drain well. Tip the parsley into a cloth and squeeze to eliminate all the water.

Put the cream and shallots into a saucepan and bring to the boil, then let bubble until reduced by one-third. Add the parsley and bubble for 2 minutes, stirring continuously with a wooden spoon.

Take the pan off the heat, add the boiling milk and stir. Tip the mixture into a blender and purée for 2–3 minutes until very smooth, then rub through a drum sieve into a bowl, using a plastic scraper. Season to taste with salt and pepper and serve hot. If necessary you can reheat this coulis, but do not let it boil.

This coulis is delicious served in little ramekins or egg coddlers, topped with a few snails sautéed in noisette butter. It is also excellent with grilled veal escalopes.

Any sauce accompanying fish must, above all, be light and only mildly flavoured with a hint of spice, or with the tenderest of fresh herbs, such as chervil or finely snipped flat-leaf parsley. Subtlety is the key, as the sauce needs to complement the fish, without disguising its delicate fragrance or overpowering its natural flavours. As always, the fish will be best appreciated if it is relatively lightly cooked. Shellfish, on the other hand, has much firmer flesh and calls for more robust sauces with greater character and less restrained seasoning. It goes without saying that shellfish, like fish, must never be overcooked otherwise their texture will be ruined. White wine and Champagne are key ingredients in many sauces that accompany fish and shellfish, and now and then I like to add a little vermouth or dessert wine. The cooking juices from mussels, clams, oysters, etc. can be used in small amounts – they enhance and intensify the flavour of a sauce in a most delicious way. When fish stock is included in a sauce, it lends harmony and balance, and the flavour is inclined to linger delectably in the mouth... a good reason for having some to hand.

sauces for
fish & seafood

600ml fish stock (page 30)
for the clarification
500g very ripe tomatoes, chopped
1 small red pepper, cored, deseeded and
  very thinly sliced
50g basil leaves, coarsely chopped
4 egg whites
8 peppercorns, crushed
salt and freshly ground pepper

Mix the ingredients for the clarification together thoroughly in a bowl.

Pour the fish stock into a saucepan and add the clarification mixture.

Bring to the boil over a medium heat, stirring occasionally with a wooden spoon.

serves 6

As soon as the liquid boils, reduce the heat and bubble very gently for 20 minutes.

Pass the clarified fumet through a fine-meshed conical sieve, season with salt and pepper to taste and serve.

Steamed fillets of fish with delicate flesh, such as red mullet, John Dory or sea bream, are delicious served in a deep plate, bathed with a ladleful of this summery fumet – redolent with the aromas of tomatoes and basil (illustrated on page 169). If you wish, sprinkle over some finely shredded basil.

vermouth sauce

serves 4

An excellent sauce to accompany braised white fish, as well as scallops and other shellfish.

40g shallot, finely chopped
1 thyme sprig
½ bay leaf
100ml Noilly Prat or dry vermouth
300ml fish stock (page 30)
2 tbsp double cream
pinch of paprika
60g butter, well chilled and diced
salt and freshly ground pepper

Put the shallot, thyme, bay leaf and vermouth into a saucepan and let bubble to reduce by one-third over a high heat.

Pour in the fish stock and cook over a medium heat for 10 minutes, then add the cream. Reduce the sauce over a high heat until it is thick enough to coat the back of a spoon.

Remove the thyme and bay leaf, then whisk in the paprika and turn the heat down to low, making sure that the sauce does not boil. Whisk in the butter, a little at a time, then season to taste with salt and pepper.

Transfer the sauce to a blender and whiz for 30 seconds until foamy, then serve immediately.

serves 4

Serve with pan-fried trout, whiting, monkfish and other fish, alongside some sautéed button mushrooms and baby onions.

250ml fish stock (page 30)
50g button mushrooms, thinly sliced
400ml velouté sauce made with fish stock (page 66)
50g butter, chilled and diced
salt
cayenne pepper

Put the fish stock and mushrooms into a saucepan and cook over a medium heat until the liquid has reduced by half.

Add the fish velouté and let the sauce bubble gently for 10 minutes, then pass it through a fine-meshed conical sieve into a clean pan.

Off the heat, whisk in the butter, a little at a time. Season the sauce to taste with salt and cayenne pepper.

I sometimes finish this sauce with 100g langoustine butter (page 132), in place of the 50g chilled butter. This makes it very delicate and perfect for serving with sea bass.

red matelote sauce For a red matelote, use fish stock made with red rather than white wine and substitute veal stock (page 26) for the velouté to give the sauce a deep amber colour.

champagne sauce

serves 6-8

This sauce is perfect for poached white fish, such as John Dory, turbot or sole. You can substitute sparkling white wine for the Champagne, but the sauce will not taste quite as good.

50g butter
60g shallots, very finely sliced
60g button mushrooms, finely sliced
400ml Champagne
300ml fish stock (page 30)
350ml double cream
salt and freshly ground white pepper

Melt 20g butter in a saucepan. Add the sliced shallots and sweat them for 1 minute, without colouring. Add the mushrooms and cook for a further 2 minutes, stirring continuously with a wooden spatula.

Pour in the Champagne and reduce by one-third over a medium heat. Add the fish stock and reduce the sauce by half.

Pour in the cream and let the sauce bubble to reduce until it lightly coats the back of a spoon. Pass it through a fine-meshed conical sieve into a clean pan.

Whisk in the remaining butter, a piece at a time, then season the sauce to taste with salt and pepper.

For a lighter texture, whiz the sauce in a blender for 1 minute before serving.

I like to add a handful of cooked, peeled shrimps to this sauce before spooning it over delicate white fish to enhance the flavour and appearance of the dish.

claret sauce

serves 8

300ml full-bodied red wine (preferably Claret)
200ml veal stock (page 26)
300ml fish stock (page 30), made with red wine
50g shallots, finely sliced
60g button mushrooms, finely sliced
1 small bouquet garni
50ml double cream
200g butter, chilled and diced
salt and freshly ground pepper

Pour the red wine and both stocks into a saucepan and add the sliced shallots, mushrooms and bouquet garni. Bring to the boil over a medium heat and let bubble to reduce until slightly syrupy.

Remove the bouquet garni, add the cream and let the sauce bubble for a minute or so, then strain it through a fine-meshed conical sieve into a clean saucepan.

Whisk in the butter, a piece at a time, until the sauce is rich and glossy. Season to taste and serve hot.

This characterful sauce makes a wonderful base for pink-fleshed fish, such as salmon, red mullet or tuna escalopes. Pan-fry the fish at the last moment, pour the sauce on to the plate and place the fish on top.

This simple, classic sauce goes well with any red- or white-fleshed fish.
I particularly enjoy it served with skate and dogfish.

60g butter
60g shallots, very finely chopped
200ml dry white wine
150ml fish stock (page 30)
400ml velouté sauce made with fish stock
    (page 66)
juice of ½ lemon
salt and freshly ground pepper
2 tbsp chopped parsley

Melt 20g butter in a saucepan, add the chopped shallots and sweat them gently
for 1 minute. Pour in the white wine and fish stock and cook over a medium heat
until the liquid has reduced by half.

Add the fish velouté and simmer gently for 20 minutes. The sauce should be
thick enough to coat the back of a spoon lightly. If it is not, cook it for a further
5–10 minutes.

Turn off the heat and whisk in the remaining butter, a small piece at a time,
followed by the lemon juice. Season the sauce with salt and pepper to taste, stir
in the chopped parsley and serve immediately.

tarragon bercy Replace the chopped parsley with 1 tbsp finely
snipped tarragon.

serves 6

55g butter
35g plain flour
150g button mushrooms, thinly sliced
300ml sweet white wine (Sauternes
   or Barsac)
600ml fish stock (page 30)
150ml double cream
80g pistachio butter (page 128), diced
salt and freshly ground pepper

Melt 35g of the butter in a heavy-based saucepan. Off the heat, stir in the flour and then cook, stirring, for 4–5 minutes, until the roux is pale hazelnut brown in colour. Let cool.

Melt the remaining 20g butter in a saucepan, add the mushrooms and sweat gently for 2 minutes. Pour in the white wine and bubble to reduce by one-third. Add the fish stock and bring to the boil. Whisk in the cooled roux, a little at a time. Cook the sauce at a very gentle bubble for 30 minutes, whisking and skimming occasionally.

Add the cream and cook until the sauce lightly coats the back of a spoon. Whisk in the pistachio butter, a piece at a time, and season to taste. Pass the sauce through a fine-meshed conical sieve. Serve at once, or keep warm in a bain-marie briefly.

I like to serve this sauce with poached or steamed fillets of sole, salmon, sea bass, turbot or John Dory.

Tamarind sauce is superb with steamed firm-fleshed fish, such as halibut or monkfish – this quantity is sufficient for a fish weighing 750g–1kg.

2 tbsp groundnut oil
4 spring onions, cut into julienne about
  3cm long
3 garlic cloves, crushed to a purée
2 tbsp finely grated fresh root ginger

2 tbsp light soy sauce
1 tbsp palm sugar
2 tbsp tamarind paste
1 tbsp fish sauce
10 black peppercorns, crushed

Heat the groundnut oil in a frying pan, add the spring onions and sauté over a medium heat until softened. Add the garlic and ginger, reduce the heat to low and cook for 2 minutes.

Add the remaining ingredients to the pan and simmer gently, stirring occasionally, for a further 2 minutes.

Transfer the sauce to a bowl and cover with cling film, piercing it in a few places. Leave to stand for about 20 minutes before serving.

My favourite way to cook and serve the fish is to steam it on a bed of shredded lettuce, then tip the sauce over the fish and serve it straight away. In winter, I sometimes coat the fish in flour and pan-fry it, a pleasing variation that produces a lovely, crisp skin.

A fresh-tasting sauce to serve with grilled scallops,
lightly poached oysters or pan-fried fillets of sea bass or bream.
It is extremely light, almost like a bouillon.

400g very fresh watercress
100g butter
500ml vegetable stock (page 33)
15g soft green peppercorns
salt and freshly ground pepper

Cut off and discard the thicker watercress stalks, retaining only the most slender
stems. Melt 30g of the butter in a saucepan. Add the watercress and sweat over
a low heat for 3 minutes, stirring continuously with a spatula.

Add the vegetable stock and green peppercorns, increase the heat to medium and
cook for 10 minutes.

Turn off the heat and leave the sauce to infuse for 10 minutes, then whiz using
a blender for 2 minutes.

Pass the sauce through a fine-meshed conical sieve into a clean saucepan, rubbing
it through with the back of a ladle.

Reheat until gently bubbling, then take the pan off the heat and whisk in the
remaining butter, a knob at a time. Season with salt and pepper to taste. Serve hot.

nantua sauce

serves 8

An excellent sauce for scallops, langoustines and any white fish with delicate, firm flesh.

80g butter
60g shallots, very finely sliced
60g button mushrooms, very finely sliced
16 crayfish or langoustine heads, raw
  or cooked, roughly chopped
2 tbsp Cognac
150ml dry white wine
300ml fish stock (page 30)

1 small bouquet garni, including
  1 or 2 tarragon sprigs
80g ripe tomatoes, peeled and deseeded
pinch of cayenne pepper
salt and freshly ground pepper
300ml double cream
a little finely snipped tarragon, to serve
  (optional)

Melt 40g butter in a shallow saucepan over a low heat. Add the sliced shallots and mushrooms and sweat for 1 minute. Add the crayfish or langoustine heads to the pan, increase the heat and fry briskly for 2–3 minutes, stirring continuously with a spatula.

Pour in the Cognac and ignite with a match. Once the flames have died down, add the white wine and reduce by half, then pour in the fish stock. Bring to the boil, then lower the heat so that the sauce bubbles gently. Add the bouquet garni, tomatoes, cayenne and a smidgeon of salt and cook for 30 minutes.

Stir in the cream and let the sauce bubble for another 10 minutes. Discard the bouquet garni. Transfer the contents of the pan to a blender and whiz for 2 minutes.

Strain the sauce through a fine-meshed conical sieve into a clean saucepan, rubbing it through with the back of a ladle. Bring the sauce back to the boil and season with salt and pepper to taste.

Off the heat, whisk in the remaining butter, a little at a time, until the sauce is smooth and glossy. It is now ready to serve. A little finely snipped tarragon added at the last moment will enhance the flavour.

seaspray sauce

serves 6

This sauce has a real tang of the sea. It is excellent served with braised fish, such as turbot or halibut, or with a fish pie.

20g butter
40g shallot, chopped
200ml fish stock (page 30)
150ml dry white wine
20g mixed dried aromatics, ground or
    pulverised, comprising equal quantities of:
    lavender flowers, dill seeds, lime flowers,
    juniper berries, coriander seeds,
    red pimento and lemon grass

6 sheets of dried edible seaweed
200ml double cream
6 medium oysters, shelled, with their juices
salt and freshly ground pepper

Melt the butter in a saucepan, add the shallot and sweat it gently for 1 minute. Pour in the fish stock and white wine, then add the mixed aromatics and seaweed and cook over a medium heat until the liquid has reduced by half.

Pour in the cream and add the oysters together with their juices. Let the sauce bubble for 5 minutes. Transfer the contents of the saucepan to a blender and whiz for 1 minute.

Pass the sauce through a fine-meshed conical sieve into a small saucepan and stand it in a bain-marie. Season to taste with salt and pepper and serve immediately, or keep the sauce warm in the bain-marie for a few minutes if necessary.

serves 6

60g butter
30g plain flour
100g button mushrooms, thinly sliced
1 thyme sprig
500ml fish stock, cooled (page 30)
50ml mussel juices (optional)
200ml double cream
3 egg yolks
juice of ½ lemon
salt and freshly ground white pepper

Melt 30g butter in a heavy-based saucepan, then take off the heat and stir in the flour. Return to a medium-low heat and cook for 2–3 minutes, stirring constantly, to make a white roux.

Meanwhile, melt the remaining 30g butter in another saucepan over a low heat. Add the mushrooms and thyme and sweat them for 2 minutes, then stir in the hot roux.

Gradually pour in the fish stock and mussel juices, if using, mixing with a small whisk. Bring to the boil, still whisking, and let the sauce bubble gently for 20 minutes, stirring it with the whisk every 5 minutes.

Meanwhile, mix the cream with the egg yolks. Stir the mixture into the sauce with the lemon juice and let it continue to bubble gently for another 10 minutes.

Season to taste with salt and white pepper. Pass the sauce through a fine-meshed conical sieve and serve immediately.

The classic sauce for *sole à la normande*, this goes well with most white fish. The addition of mussel cooking juices makes it extra special.

Perfect with shelled mussels cooked *à la marinière*, this is also very good with poached cod or halibut, rice pilaf and pasta.

50g butter
60g onions, finely chopped
2 tsp curry powder
15g plain flour
500ml cooking liquor from mussels and
   other shellfish, such as clams, cooled
1 small bouquet garni
150ml double cream
salt and freshly ground pepper

Melt the butter in a saucepan, add the onions and sweat over a low heat for 3 minutes. Add the curry powder, then the flour, stir with a wooden spoon and cook for another 3 minutes.

Pour in the cold shellfish juices, add the bouquet garni and bring to the boil. Let the sauce bubble very gently for 20 minutes, stirring every 5 minutes.

Add the cream, let bubble for another minute or so, then discard the bouquet garni. Season the sauce to taste with salt and pepper. Serve immediately.

seafood sauce with saffron

serves 4

This creamy sauce will enhance lightly poached seafood – especially langoustines and lobster – or ribbon pasta tossed with shellfish.

350ml cooking juices from shellfish (mussels,
   scallops, oysters, clams, etc.)
250ml fish stock (page 30) or cooking
   juices from langoustines
pinch of saffron threads
200ml double cream
salt and freshly ground white pepper

Combine the shellfish juices and fish stock in a saucepan and bring to the boil over a high heat. Let bubble until reduced by two-thirds.

Add the saffron and cream and bubble for 5 minutes until the sauce is thick enough to lightly coat the back of a spoon. Pass it through a conical sieve and season with salt and pepper to taste. Serve at once.

NOTE For a lighter sauce, you can substitute fromage frais for the double cream, but do not allow the sauce to boil. Heat it to 90°C and whisk well before serving, or, better still, give it a quick whiz in a blender.

This is delicious with almost all poached, steamed or braised fish. I also enjoy it poured over quartered hard-boiled eggs.

20g butter
20g plain flour
600ml fish stock, cooled (page 30)
200ml double cream
60g shrimp butter (page 131)
salt and freshly ground pepper
pinch of cayenne pepper
60g cooked and peeled pink or brown shrimps

First make a blond roux. Melt the butter in a heavy-based saucepan, then take off the heat and stir in the flour. Return to a medium heat and cook for 4–5 minutes, stirring continuously, until the roux is pale hazelnut brown in colour.

Whisk in the fish stock and bring to the boil, still whisking, then immediately reduce the heat to very low. Cook gently for 30 minutes, whisking every 10 minutes and making sure that the whisk goes right into the bottom of the pan. Use a spoon to remove any skin that forms on this sauce as it cooks.

Pour in the cream and let the sauce bubble for another 10 minutes. Now reduce the heat to as low as possible (use a heat diffuser if you have one) and whisk in the shrimp butter, a little at a time. Season the sauce with salt and pepper and spice it up with cayenne to taste. Pass it through a fine-meshed conical sieve, then add the shrimp tails and serve immediately.

A small splash of dry sherry added to the sauce just before serving gives it another dimension.

thermidor sauce

serves 6

This famous companion to lobster thermidor works with most crustaceans. It tastes wonderful mixed with crabmeat and served *au gratin*.

40g shallot, very finely chopped
200ml fish stock (page 30)
200ml dry white wine
300ml béchamel sauce (page 56)
100ml double cream
1 tsp strong Dijon mustard

1 tsp English mustard powder, dissolved
  in a few drops of water
50g butter, well chilled and diced
salt
pinch of cayenne pepper
1 tbsp finely snipped tarragon (optional)

Combine the shallot, fish stock and white wine in a saucepan and let bubble until the liquid has reduced by two-thirds. Add the béchamel and cook the sauce over a low heat for 20 minutes, stirring every 5 minutes.

Pour in the cream, let bubble for 5 minutes, then add both mustards and cook for another 2 minutes.

Turn off the heat and whisk the butter into the sauce, a piece at a time. Season with salt and a good pinch of cayenne to taste. Finally add the tarragon, if using, and serve immediately.

If you wish, add a teaspoonful of Cognac to the sauce at the end of cooking.

américaine sauce

serves 6

This classic supreme sauce takes time to prepare, but is well worth the effort. Serve it with firm-fleshed fish, such as poached turbot, or a fish soufflé.

1 live lobster, 800g–1kg, rinsed
small pinch of cayenne pepper
salt and freshly ground pepper
100ml groundnut oil
4 tbsp very finely diced carrots
2 tbsp very finely diced shallot or onion
2 unpeeled garlic cloves, smashed
50ml Cognac or Armagnac

300ml dry white wine
300ml fish stock (page 30)
200g very ripe tomatoes, peeled, deseeded
 and chopped
1 bouquet garni, containing 1 tarragon sprig
60g butter
10g plain flour
75ml double cream (optional)

Plunge the lobster into a large pan of boiling water for 45 seconds. Lift out and place on a board. Separate the head and body and cut the claw joints and tail into rings across the articulations. Split the head lengthways and remove the gritty sac close to the feelers, and the greyish membranes. Scrape out the greenish coral from the head and reserve in a bowl. Season the lobster with cayenne, salt and pepper.

Heat the groundnut oil in a deep sauté pan over a high heat. When it is sizzling, add the lobster pieces and sauté until the shell turns bright red and the flesh is lightly coloured. Remove with a slotted spoon to a plate. Discard most of the oil in the pan.

Sweat the carrots and shallot in the pan until soft but not coloured. Add the garlic and return the lobster to the pan. Pour in the Cognac and ignite. Once the flames have died down, pour in the wine and stock. Add the tomatoes, bouquet garni and a little salt. As it comes to the boil, lower the heat and cook gently for 15 minutes.

Remove and reserve the claws and rings of lobster tail containing the meat. Cook the sauce at a gentle bubble for a further 30 minutes, skimming once or twice.

With a fork, mash the lobster coral with the butter and flour, then add to the sauce, a little at a time. Cook for 5 minutes, then add the cream, if using, and pass through a fine-meshed conical strainer, pressing with the back of a ladle. Season to taste.

For a lighter texture, whiz the sauce in a blender for 1 minute. Remove the reserved lobster meat from the shell, dice it and add to the sauce just before serving.

The meat course always signifies the high point of a meal, making the effort you put into an accompanying sauce all the more worthwhile. This chapter offers a rich assortment – more than a dozen sauces to choose from – but the choice is all-important. Each sauce has a specific role and care must be taken to ensure that the sauce you select is compatible with the meat you are serving. As a general rule, beef calls for a sauce that is stronger, smoother and richer than a sauce for lamb or veal, which should have a more delicate flavour and texture. I have also included a selection of simple 'jus', which are invariably very light in character and serve to enhance roast meats. They can be prepared in just a few minutes, while your meat is resting. For an original, healthy sauce, I urge you to try my rocket sauce with piquant horseradish (page 214). It has a distinctive flavour and goes wonderfully with cold meats.

sauces for meat, poultry & game

lamb jus with rosemary

A light, easy-to-prepare jus that goes beautifully with roast lamb.

200g carrots, cut into rounds
250g onions, cut into large dice
3 medium garlic cloves, peeled
6 black peppercorns, crushed
2 bay leaves
1–2 fresh rosemary sprigs
200ml red wine (preferably Grenache)
salt and freshly ground pepper

Continue to roast, basting from time to time and stirring the vegetables and herbs around to ensure they colour but do not burn. When the lamb is cooked, lift it on to a rack over a platter, partially cover with foil and leave to rest in a warm place.

Preheat the oven to 220°C/Gas 7. Put your lamb joint in a roasting tin and roast until lightly browned, about 20 minutes. Lower the oven setting according to the size and cut of meat and take the roasting tin out. Scatter the carrots, onions, garlic cloves, peppercorns and herbs around the lamb and return to the oven.

Using a spoon, remove the excess fat from the surface of the juices in the roasting tin.

Now pour in the red wine to deglaze. Cook over a low heat until reduced by two-thirds.

Strain the jus through a fine-meshed conical sieve into a saucepan, lightly pressing the vegetables and herbs with the back of a small ladle to extract as much flavour and juice as possible. Add any juices from the rested meat and taste for seasoning, adding salt and pepper as necessary. Keep the jus warm until ready to serve the lamb.

Add 3 tbsp water (or use chicken stock) and cook for a further 5 minutes, stirring from time to time with a wooden spoon and crushing the garlic cloves with a fork. The soft garlic flesh will flavour the jus and thicken it slightly.

chicken jus with savory

serves 6

This flavourful jus is perfect for roast chicken, poussin or guinea fowl. I like to serve green beans or pasta as an accompaniment, as they are delicious dunked in the liquor. If preferred, you can use fresh tarragon instead of savory; it is equally compatible with poultry dishes.

200g carrots, cut into rounds
150g onions, cut into dice
1 medium potato, peeled and cut into 8 pieces
1 thyme sprig

2 unpeeled medium garlic cloves
150ml dry white wine
50g savory sprigs
150ml chicken stock (page 28) or water
salt and freshly ground pepper

Preheat the oven to 220°C/Gas 7. Put your bird(s) in a roasting tin and roast in the oven until lightly browned, about 20 minutes. Lower the oven setting to 190°C/Gas 5 and take the roasting tin out. Distribute the carrots, onions, potato, thyme and garlic around the bird. Return to the oven and roast until cooked through, basting from time to time using a spoon, and stirring the vegetables around so that they take on some colour without burning.

When the bird is cooked through, remove the legs and breasts, with wing attached. Put them on a warm plate, partially cover with foil and leave to rest in a warm place. Break the carcass up, using poultry shears or a small cleaver. Using a spoon, skim the fat from the roasting tin and add the carcass pieces and bones to the tin.

Pour in the white wine to deglaze, add the savory and cook over a medium heat for 10 minutes. Crush the potato pieces with a fork to bind the jus, add the chicken stock and cook for a further 10 minutes.

Strain through a fine-meshed conical sieve into a saucepan, pressing down on the bones and vegetables with the back of a small ladle to extract as much flavour and juice as possible. Season to taste with salt and pepper. Keep the jus warm until ready to serve with the rested poultry.

quick sauce for game birds

serves 4

carcasses of 2 roasted wild duck or snipe,
  or 4 wood pigeons
50ml Cognac or Armagnac
150ml red wine
450ml vegetable stock (page 33)
5 juniper berries, crushed
1 thyme sprig
½ bay leaf
4 tbsp double cream
salt and freshly ground pepper

Chop the game carcasses, place in a saucepan and heat them through, then add the Cognac and ignite it. When the flames have died down, pour in the red wine and let it bubble over a high heat to reduce by half.

Pour in the vegetable stock and add the juniper berries, thyme and bay leaf. Cook briskly until the liquid has reduced by half, then add the cream and let bubble for another 3 minutes.

Pass the sauce through a fine-meshed conical sieve into a clean pan, reheat gently and season with salt and pepper to taste. Serve immediately.

This sauce has a lovely mild, gamey flavour, as it absorbs the savour of the carcasses during its brief cooking. Serve with roasted game birds.

serves 6

Perfect with roast poultry, this light gravy is also good with spinach,
braised chicory and salsify.

3 tbsp groundnut oil
1kg chicken wings, coarsely chopped
100g carrots, chopped
100g onions, chopped
200ml dry white wine
5 juniper berries, crushed
1 garlic clove, crushed
25g thyme sprigs
salt and freshly ground pepper

Heat the groundnut oil in a deep frying pan, put in the chicken wings and fry over a high heat until golden brown, stirring occasionally with a wooden spoon.

Pour off the oil and the fat released by the chicken, then add the carrots and onions to the pan. Stir with a wooden spoon and sweat gently for 3 minutes.

Pour in the white wine and let bubble to reduce the liquid by half. Add 1 litre cold water, the juniper berries, garlic and thyme, and season sparingly with salt and pepper. Bring the sauce to a simmer and let bubble gently for 45 minutes, skimming as often as necessary.

Pass the sauce through a conical sieve into a clean pan and reheat; it is now ready to serve. For a more concentrated flavour, reduce the sauce over a medium heat to taste.

This gravy will keep in a covered container in the fridge for several days; it can also be frozen for up to a month.

lamb gravy scented with lavender honey

serves 8

A lovely sauce to serve with grilled lamb chops or a roast leg of
lamb accompanied by creamy mashed potato.

4 tbsp groundnut oil
1kg neck or scrag end of lamb on the
    bone, coarsely chopped
50g honey (preferably lavender)
100g carrots, coarsely chopped
100g onions, coarsely chopped
200ml red wine

1 bouquet garni
6 peppercorns, crushed
1 garlic clove, crushed
1 marmande tomato, peeled, deseeded
    and chopped
salt and freshly ground pepper

Heat the groundnut oil in a deep frying pan, put in the lamb and fry briskly until
browned all over. Pour off the oil and the fat released by the lamb.

Using a palette knife, spread the honey over the pieces of lamb, then add the carrots
and onions to the pan. Stir with a wooden spoon and sweat gently for 3 minutes.

Pour in the red wine, stirring to deglaze, and cook over a medium heat for 5 minutes.
Pour in 1.25 litres water and add the bouquet garni, peppercorns, garlic and tomato.
Season sparingly with salt and pepper, and bring to a simmer. Let the sauce bubble
gently for 1 hour, skimming the surface whenever necessary.

Pass the sauce through a conical sieve into a clean pan; it is now ready to serve.
Alternatively, for a more concentrated aroma, reduce the sauce for a little longer.

The gravy will keep in a covered container in the fridge for a few days, or it can
be frozen for up to a month.

serves 4

250g chicken wings and necks
2 tbsp groundnut oil
60g shallots, diced
80g carrots, diced
60g celery, diced
4 star anise, coarsely chopped

2 tbsp Curaçao
200ml chicken stock (page 28)
200ml veal stock (page 26)
30g butter, chilled and diced
salt and freshly ground pepper

Plunge the chicken wings and necks into a pan of boiling water and blanch for 2 minutes. Drain and refresh in cold water, then drain thoroughly.

Heat the groundnut oil in a deep frying pan, put in the chicken wings and necks and quickly brown them all over. Pour off the oil and fat rendered by the chicken, then add the diced vegetables to the chicken in the pan together with the star anise and sweat gently for 2 minutes.

Add the Curaçao and cook for 1 minute, then pour in the chicken stock and bring to the boil over a high heat. Bubble vigorously to reduce the stock by half.

Now pour in the veal stock and lower the heat. Simmer gently for 20 minutes.

Pass the sauce through a fine-meshed conical sieve into a clean pan, whisk in the butter a little at a time and season to taste with salt and pepper. Serve immediately.

This sauce has a very light consistency, almost like a thin gravy. I like to serve it with roast or pan-fried poussin or pigeon.

buccaneer's sauce

serves 8

100g butter, half of it chilled and diced
60g shallots or small onions, thinly sliced
40g fresh root ginger, peeled and finely grated
100g banana, peeled and sliced into rounds
6 tbsp raspberry vinegar (page 119), or
   use ready-made
400ml veal stock (page 26)
salt and freshly ground pepper

Melt the non-chilled half of the butter in a saucepan. Add the sliced shallots and sweat over a medium heat for 1 minute. Add the ginger and cook, stirring, until the shallots are very lightly coloured.

Add the banana and cook, stirring with a spatula, over a low heat for 2 minutes until it softens and begins to disintegrate. Immediately add the raspberry vinegar and continue to stir over a low heat for another 2 minutes.

Add the veal stock and simmer gently for 20 minutes, then pass the sauce through a fine-meshed sieve into another pan.

Whisk in the remaining butter, a piece at a time, until the sauce is smooth and glossy. Season with salt and pepper to taste. Serve at once.

I serve this sauce with veal chops garnished with slices of banana pan-fried in butter. You can serve roast chicken and turkey as well as roast veal in the same way.

This wonderful sauce looks as good as it tastes. It is delicious with any cut of beef, especially entrecôte, rib and sirloin. Remember to soak the beef marrow in advance.

40g shallots, finely chopped
8 white peppercorns, crushed
200ml red wine (preferably Claret)
300ml veal stock (page 26)
1 small bouquet garni
200g beef marrow, soaked in iced water
    for 4 hours
salt and freshly ground pepper
30g butter, chilled and diced

Put the shallots, crushed peppercorns and red wine in a saucepan and set over a high heat. Let bubble until the wine has reduced by one-third.

Add the veal stock and bouquet garni and bubble gently for about 20 minutes, or until the sauce has reduced and thickened enough to lightly coat the back of a spoon. Pass it through a fine-meshed conical sieve into another saucepan.

Drain the beef marrow and cut it into small pieces or rounds. Place in a small saucepan, cover with a little cold water and salt lightly. Bring to the boil over a medium heat. Immediately turn off the heat, leave the marrow for 30 seconds, then drain it carefully.

Season the sauce with salt and pepper to taste. Whisk in the butter, a piece at a time, then add the well-drained beef marrow. Taste and adjust the seasoning. Serve immediately.

chasseur sauce

serves 8

100g butter, half of it chilled and diced
200g button mushrooms, wiped and
 finely sliced
40g shallot, finely chopped
400ml dry white wine
400ml veal stock (page 26)
1 tbsp snipped flat-leaf parsley
1 tsp snipped tarragon
salt and freshly ground pepper

Melt the non-chilled half of the butter in a shallow pan, add the mushrooms and cook over a medium heat for 1 minute. Add the shallot and cook for another minute, taking care not to let it colour.

Tip the mushroom and shallot mixture into a fine-meshed conical sieve to drain off the cooking butter, then return to the shallow pan. Add the white wine and let bubble over a medium heat until reduced by half.

Pour in the veal stock and cook gently for 10–15 minutes until the sauce has reduced and thickened enough to lightly coat the back of a spoon.

Take the pan off the heat and whisk in the remaining butter, a piece at a time, along with the snipped herbs. Season to taste with salt and pepper. The sauce is now ready to serve.

This light mushroom and white wine sauce is quick to make. It goes very well with poultry and veal.

bigarade sauce

serves 6

I love to serve this sauce with slices of pan-fried calf's liver
or sliced grilled kidneys. For a classic sauce to accompany
duck *à l'orange*, I include duck wings.

1 lemon
3 oranges
45g caster sugar
3 tbsp red wine vinegar
300g duck wings (optional)
a little oil for frying (optional)
700ml veal stock (page 26)
salt and freshly ground pepper

Finely pare the zest from the lemon and two of the oranges and reserve. Squeeze
the juice from all of the citrus fruit and set aside.

Put the sugar and wine vinegar into a deep frying pan and dissolve over a very low
heat. Continue to cook until you have a deep golden caramel.

If using duck wings, brown them quickly in a little oil in another frying pan, turning
to colour all over.

As soon as the vinegar syrup has formed a caramel, pour in the veal stock and orange
and lemon juices and add the duck wings, if using. Bring to the boil, lower the heat and
cook gently for 45 minutes, skimming the surface as necessary. The sauce should be
thick enough to lightly coat the back of a spoon. If it is not, cook for a little longer.

In the meantime, cut the citrus zests into fine julienne. Add to a pan of boiling
water and blanch for 1 minute. Drain thoroughly.

Pass the sauce through a fine-meshed conical sieve into a clean pan and season with
salt and pepper to taste, then add the orange and lemon zests. The sauce is now ready
to serve. If you are not serving the sauce immediately, keep it warm in a bain-marie
but only add the zests when you are about to serve.

This homely piquant sauce is delicious with pork chops and mashed potatoes. I prefer it to have a slightly thick consistency, which complements the texture of pork.

30g butter
60g onions, finely chopped
100ml dry white wine
300ml veal stock (page 26)
1 tbsp strong Dijon mustard
40g beurre manié (see below)
salt and freshly ground pepper
30g cornichons, cut into long, thin strips

Melt the butter in a small saucepan, add the onions and sweat gently without colouring for 1 minute. Pour in the white wine and let bubble over a medium heat to reduce by half.

Add the veal stock and bubble the sauce gently until it is thick enough to lightly coat the back of a spoon. Whisk in the mustard and the beurre manié, a little at a time, and cook for another 2 minutes. Season with salt and pepper to taste.

Pass the sauce through a fine-meshed conical sieve into a small pan containing the cornichons. Serve it immediately, or keep warm for a few minutes in a bain-marie set over a low heat.

A beurre manié is a mixture of equal parts soft butter and flour, mixed together with a fork, which can be used to thicken an overly liquid or thin sauce very swiftly at the end of cooking. It should be incorporated into the sauce a small piece at a time.

périgueux sauce

serves 6

400ml veal stock (page 26)
50ml truffle juice (bottled or ideally the
   cooking juices from fresh truffles)
20g truffles, finely chopped or sliced
   into discs
40g butter, chilled and diced
salt and freshly ground pepper

Bring the veal stock to the boil in a small saucepan and let bubble over a medium heat to reduce until it is thick enough to lightly coat the back of a spoon.

Add the truffle juice and cook for another 5 minutes. Add the chopped truffles and let the sauce bubble briefly.

Take the pan off the heat and add the butter, a piece at a time, swirling and rotating the pan to incorporate it. Season the sauce with salt and pepper to taste and serve immediately.

This sauce is excellent served with little hot pies or pâtés en croûte, with beef tournedos or pan-fried saddle of lamb, and of course on pasta. To make it richer and more unctuous, whisk in 50g foie gras butter (page 128) just before serving, in place of the chilled butter.

211

zingara sauce

serves 6

400ml veal stock (page 26)
1 tbsp cooked tomato coulis (page 163)
30g butter
60g button mushrooms, wiped and
  cut into batons
50ml dry white wine
30g lean ham, cut into batons
30g cooked ox tongue, cut into batons
40g fresh or preserved truffle, cut into batons
2 tbsp Madeira
salt and cayenne pepper

Put the veal stock and tomato coulis in a saucepan and bring to the boil. Let bubble over a medium heat until reduced by two-thirds, then pass the liquid through a fine-meshed conical sieve into a bowl and set aside.

In another saucepan, melt the butter, add the mushrooms and sweat them gently for 30 seconds. Pour in the white wine and reduce it almost completely.

Add the ham, tongue and truffle, mix delicately with a wooden spoon, then pour in the Madeira and cook at a bare simmer for 2 minutes.

Add the reduced veal stock and simmer for another 5 minutes. Season the sauce with salt and cayenne to taste and serve at once.

Serve this fine, delicate sauce with pan-fried or grilled poultry or with veal escalopes.

serves 4

This sauce is excellent with grilled brochettes of lamb, or with pan-fried veal tournedos or calf's liver.

250g chicken wings, blanched, refreshed
 and drained
2 tbsp groundnut oil
60g carrots, chopped
60g onions, chopped
50ml white wine vinegar
400ml chicken stock (page 28)

80g tomatoes, peeled, deseeded
 and chopped
1 small bouquet garni, including
 a tarragon sprig
100ml double cream
1 tsp five-spice powder
salt and freshly ground pepper

Plunge the chicken wings into a pan of boiling water and blanch for 2 minutes. Drain and refresh in cold water, then drain thoroughly and pat dry.

Heat the groundnut oil in a deep frying pan, add the chicken wings and brown over a high heat.

Pour off the oil and fat from the chicken, then add the carrots and onions to the pan and sweat them for 2 minutes. Off the heat, sprinkle on the wine vinegar and leave to stand for 1 minute.

Add the chicken stock, tomatoes and bouquet garni. Bring to the boil, then lower the heat and cook, skimming the surface whenever necessary, until the sauce lightly coats the back of a spoon.

Add the cream and five-spice powder and bubble gently for 2 minutes. Pass the sauce through a fine-meshed conical sieve and season with salt and pepper to taste. Keep it warm in a bain-marie or serve immediately.

rocket sauce with horseradish

serves 8

60g rocket leaves, stalks removed
1 tbsp Dijon mustard or
  1 tsp wasabi powder
2–3 tsp finely grated horseradish
  (preferably fresh), to taste
2 tbsp light olive oil
2 tbsp milk
juice of 1 lemon
1 garlic clove, finely crushed
150g Greek yoghurt
salt and freshly ground pepper

Put all the ingredients, except the yoghurt and seasoning, into a blender and process for 2–3 minutes until smooth.

Transfer to a large bowl and whisk in the yoghurt until combined. Season the sauce with salt and pepper to taste.

Cover with cling film and refrigerate until ready to use. This sauce keeps well for 2–3 days in the fridge, needing only a quick whisk through before serving.

This fresh-tasting, healthy sauce goes beautifully with cold meat, such as beef, pork, lamb, poultry, or a bone-in ham for a buffet or picnic. It is also excellent served with cold poached salmon or smoked trout.

olive and savory sauce

serves 4

This sauce is very thin, almost like a jus, and bursting
with the Provençal flavours of savory and olives.

100ml dry white wine
40g shallot, chopped
15g savory
6 white peppercorns, crushed
200ml lamb stock (page 29) or veal stock
   (page 26)
60g black or green olive paste (tapenade)
30g butter, chilled and diced
salt and freshly ground pepper

Combine the white wine, shallot, savory and crushed peppercorns in a small
saucepan. Set over a medium heat and let bubble to reduce the wine by half.

Pour in the stock, reduce the heat to very low and simmer gently for 20 minutes.

Whisk in the olive paste, then, still over the lowest possible heat, whisk in the
butter, a little at a time. Season the sauce to taste with salt and pepper, pass it
through a fine-meshed conical sieve and serve at once.

serves 4

150g aubergine
salt
2 tbsp olive oil
60g shallots, finely chopped
50ml red wine
300ml veal stock (page 26)
2 tbsp double cream
large pinch of paprika
1 tbsp wholegrain mustard
1 tbsp snipped tarragon

Cut the aubergine into cubes, salt lightly and leave for 15 minutes to draw out any bitter juices, then rinse and pat dry with kitchen paper.

Heat the olive oil in a saucepan, then add the chopped shallots and aubergine cubes. Cook over a medium heat, stirring with a wooden spoon, until the aubergine begins to soften. Add the red wine and let bubble for 3 minutes.

Pour in the veal stock and bubble gently for 15 minutes. Add the cream and a generous pinch of paprika, then transfer the sauce to a blender and whiz for 30 seconds.

Pass the sauce through a fine-meshed conical sieve into another saucepan, add the mustard and tarragon and bring back to the boil. Season with salt to taste and serve at once.

Tarragon and mustard add a refreshing note to this sauce, while the aubergine gives it a smooth, creamy texture. Serve it with roast rabbit, veal or pork chops. It is also a good accompaniment to a dish of broad noodles.

serves 6

40g shallots, chopped
200ml red wine (preferably Côtes du Rhône)
300ml veal stock (page 26)
14 juniper berries, crushed
2 tbsp redcurrant jelly
40g butter, chilled and diced
salt and freshly ground pepper

Put the shallots and red wine into a saucepan, bring to the boil over a medium heat and let bubble to reduce the wine by one-third.

Add the veal stock, then the juniper berries and let bubble gently for 15 minutes. Add the redcurrant jelly, stir to dissolve, then pass the sauce through a fine-meshed conical sieve into a clean pan.

Whisk in the butter, a little at a time, season to taste with salt and pepper and serve immediately.

This simple sauce is highly fragrant. It is perfect with grilled steaks or lightly cooked game, such as pan-fried fillets of hare or medallions of venison.

devil sauce

serves 4

This robust, highly scented sauce goes very well with all grilled poultry, particularly spatchcocked poussin or chicken.

2 tbsp red wine vinegar
100ml dry white wine
20 white peppercorns, crushed
50g shallots, chopped
1 bouquet garni, including 2 tarragon sprigs
400ml veal stock (page 26)
40g butter, chilled and diced
salt and freshly ground pepper
1 tbsp snipped chervil or flat-leaf parsley

Combine the wine vinegar, white wine, crushed white peppercorns, shallots and bouquet garni in a saucepan. Set over a medium heat and let bubble until the liquid has reduced down by four-fifths.

Pour in the veal stock and let bubble gently for about 20 minutes, or until the sauce is thick enough to lightly coat the back of a spoon. Pass it through a fine-meshed sieve into a clean saucepan.

Whisk the butter into the sauce, a little at a time. Season to taste with salt and pepper and add the snipped herb just before serving.

8 tbsp crunchy peanut butter
1 garlic clove, finely crushed
1 tbsp palm sugar
2 tbsp dark soy sauce
1 tbsp lemon juice
2 tbsp tamarind liquid
generous pinch of hot chilli powder
a little coconut milk, to bind the sauce

Put the peanut butter into a saucepan with 100ml water and heat gently, stirring with a wooden spoon. As soon as it starts to boil, remove from the heat and add the remaining ingredients. Stir until thoroughly mixed, then set aside until ready to use.

This sauce is best served hot or warm. It keeps well for several days in the fridge in a sealed container; just reheat it gently, preferably in a bain-marie, to serve.

Partner barbecued or grilled brochettes of pork, lamb or chicken with this flavourful satay sauce, serving it warm. You can also serve it at room temperature as a dip for crudités – carrots, celery, cucumber, etc.

Fruit can really bring a sauce to life. Selected carefully and used judiciously, it adds an element of freshness, subtlety and gentle sweetness to sauces, lending a slight hint of acidity at the same time. These are the characteristics I seek to produce in many of my sauces to pair with meat, poultry and game – notably rabbit, venison, duck breasts, pigeon and roast pork. From apples to mangoes, I engage more than a dozen varieties of fruit and these days I find I am using them more and more. Of course, from a health perspective, we should be eating plenty of fruit, so you needn't think twice about treating yourself generously to a fruit sauce. At the end of this chapter you will come across a selection of my favourite fruit chutney recipes. I love to serve these with my terrine pâtés and pâtés en croûte, and with cold meats – especially pork pies, which I adore. And, of course, they are equally delicious with a piece of good, mature Cheddar.

savoury fruity sauces & chutneys

apple sauce

serves 6

This lovely, tangy sauce is the classic accompaniment to roast pork.

500g dessert apples (preferably Cox's)
20g caster sugar
juice of ½ lemon
½ cinnamon stick, or pinch of ground cinnamon
30g butter
pinch of salt

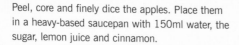

Peel, core and finely dice the apples. Place them in a heavy-based saucepan with 150ml water, the sugar, lemon juice and cinnamon.

Bring to a simmer over a medium heat, then cover and cook for about 15 minutes until the apples are tender but not dried out. Discard the cinnamon stick.

It will also complement roast partridge, pheasant,
wild duck and young wild boar.

If the sauce seems too thick, add 1–2 tbsp water
to thin it slightly. Serve warm.

Take the pan off the heat and, using a small
whisk, incorporate the butter and a pinch of salt
to make a smooth compote. The consistency will
vary according to how ripe or green the apples are.

peach sauce

serves 4

I serve this delicate, fruity sauce with roasted pigeon or young duckling. For preference, make the sauce with white peaches.

2 very ripe medium peaches
30g butter
30g caster sugar
20ml Cognac
3 tbsp red wine vinegar
100ml red wine (preferably Burgundy)

1 clove
1½ tsp fennel seeds
300ml veal stock (page 26)
40g butter, chilled and diced
salt and freshly ground pepper

To peel the peaches, lightly score around the middle, then immerse in boiling water until the skin starts to lift. Refresh in iced water, then peel, stone and cut into cubes.

Melt the butter in a frying pan, add the sugar and stir until lightly caramelised. Add the peaches, increase the heat and cook, stirring, until almost collapsed to a purée. Add the Cognac, bubble briefly, then add the wine vinegar and bubble for 1 minute. Add the red wine and spices and cook gently for 10 minutes, skimming as necessary.

Pour in the veal stock and simmer for 30 minutes, or until reduced and thickened. Strain into a clean pan and whisk in the butter, a little at a time. Season and serve.

serves 4

1 very ripe mango
2 passion fruit
2 tbsp Cognac or Armagnac
200ml veal stock (page 26)
100ml double cream
4 drops of Tabasco
salt and freshly ground pepper

Using a small knife with a flexible blade, peel the mango and cut the flesh away from the stone. Finely dice the flesh and place in a small saucepan.

Halve the passion fruit, scoop out the seeds into the saucepan and add the Cognac.

Cook over a low heat for 5 minutes, then add the veal stock and cook for another 5 minutes. Pour in the cream, add the Tabasco and let bubble for 5 minutes.

Transfer the sauce to a blender and whiz for 1 minute, then pass the sauce through a fine-meshed conical sieve into a small saucepan. Heat gently and season to taste with salt and pepper.

Serve immediately, or you can keep the sauce warm in a bain-marie for a short while if necessary.

This fruity, refreshing sauce has a light spiciness. It is particularly good with sautéed chicken or rabbit served with leaf spinach or fresh pasta.

cumberland sauce

serves 4

1 medium shallot, finely chopped
4 tbsp wine vinegar (preferably red)
12 white peppercorns, crushed
100ml veal stock (page 26)
50ml ruby port
2 tbsp redcurrant jelly
1 tsp Worcestershire sauce
juice of 1 orange
salt
finely pared zest of 1 lemon

Combine the shallot, wine vinegar and crushed peppercorns in a small saucepan. Place over a high heat and let bubble to reduce by two-thirds.

Add the veal stock, port, redcurrant jelly, Worcestershire sauce and orange juice. Quickly bring to the boil, then lower the heat and simmer gently for 20 minutes. Season with salt to taste.

Pass the sauce through a fine-meshed conical sieve into a bowl. Set aside to cool, then cover and chill in the refrigerator.

Blanch the lemon zest in boiling water for 1 minute, then drain and cut into fine julienne. Stir into the sauce just before serving.

This is a lovely accompaniment to cold meats and terrines. Serve it cold with galantines and ballotines, pork pies or any cold poultry or game. It tastes even better the day after it is made.

serves 4

60g butter
60g shallots, very finely sliced
100g button mushrooms, finely sliced
50g blackcurrants or cranberries
250ml ruby port
dried zest of ¼ orange
300ml veal stock (page 26) or game stock
   (page 32)
salt and freshly ground pepper

Melt half the butter in a small saucepan. Add the shallots and sweat until soft, then add the mushrooms and fruit and cook gently for 3–4 minutes.

Pour in the port, add the orange zest and reduce by one-third. Add the stock and simmer for 25 minutes, skimming the surface whenever necessary.

Pass the sauce through a fine-meshed conical sieve into a clean pan. Swirl in the rest of the butter, shaking and rotating the pan, then season to taste with salt and pepper. The sauce is now ready to serve.

This light sauce is excellent with pan-fried pheasant breasts and venison cutlets; I also like to serve it with roast partridge. For preference, I use blackcurrants, but since their season is short, I also make it with cranberries.

sweet and sour sauce

serves 4–6

200g green peppers
200g red peppers
2 tbsp groundnut oil
200g onions, finely diced
100g demerara sugar
100ml red wine vinegar
150ml veal stock (page 26), chicken stock
   (page 28) or vegetable stock (page 33)
salt and freshly ground pepper

Oil the peppers very lightly and grill them (under a very hot grill or in a hot oven) until the skins are blistered and blackened. Plunge the charred peppers into a bowl of iced water to cool them quickly, then remove and peel off the skins. Halve the peppers, remove the core, pith and seeds, then dice the flesh.

Gently heat the groundnut oil in a heavy-based saucepan. Add the onions and sweat for 5 minutes, stirring with a wooden spoon. Add the peppers and sweat, stirring, for another 5 minutes. Add the sugar and cook until the vegetables are lightly caramelised, stirring all the time.

Pour in the wine vinegar, stirring to deglaze the pan, and let bubble over a medium heat until the liquid has reduced by two-thirds. Add the stock and cook until the sauce is reduced and lightly coats the back of a spoon. Season with salt and pepper to taste.

Serve this sauce tepid or cold. Stored in an airtight jar in the fridge, it will keep well for 2 weeks.

The perfect dipping sauce for scampi and squid tempura, this sauce is also very good with sashimi, ham and other cold meat dishes.

pumpkin sauce with sweet spices

serves 4

With its delicate aroma of spices, this fruity sauce is perfect with fillets of wild rabbit, noisettes of young wild boar or pan-fried breast of wild duck.

500g game trimmings and/or game
  carcasses (optional)
300g deseeded pumpkin flesh
3 tbsp oil
60g shallots, finely chopped
50ml raspberry vinegar (page 119), or
  use ready-prepared

200ml sweet white wine (Sauternes or Barsac)
500ml vegetable stock (page 33)
1 bouquet garni
1 vanilla pod, split lengthways
3 star anise
40g butter, chilled and diced
salt and freshly ground pepper

Chop up the game carcasses, if using. Cut the pumpkin flesh into small cubes. Heat the oil in a deep frying pan, add the game trimmings or carcasses and briskly brown them all over.

Pour off the fat released by the game, then add the shallots and pumpkin to the pan and sweat them gently over a low heat for 3 minutes. Take off the heat and add the raspberry vinegar. After 1 minute, return to the heat and deglaze with the white wine.

Allow to simmer for 5 minutes, then add the vegetable stock, bouquet garni, vanilla and star anise. Bring to a simmer and cook very gently for 45 minutes, skimming the surface whenever necessary.

Pass the sauce through a fine-meshed conical sieve into a clean pan and simmer to reduce until thickened enough to coat the back of a spoon.

Off the heat, whisk in the butter, a little at a time. Season to taste with salt and pepper and serve at once.

6 very ripe fresh figs, each cut into 6 pieces
100ml ruby port
400ml game stock (page 32)
6 black peppercorns, crushed
1 tbsp instant coffee powder, dissolved
   in 1 tbsp hot water
40g butter, chilled and diced
salt and freshly ground pepper

Put the figs and port into a saucepan and simmer gently for 5 minutes. Pour in the game stock, add the crushed peppercorns and bring to a simmer. Let bubble gently for 25 minutes, skimming the surface from time to time.

Add the coffee, then immediately turn off the heat. Pour the sauce into a blender and whiz for 30 seconds, then pass it through a fine-meshed conical sieve into a clean pan.

Whisk the butter into the sauce, a piece at a time. Season to taste with salt and pepper and serve immediately.

This sauce is excellent with roast wild duck or wood pigeon. Fresh figs poached in red wine make a wonderful garnish. Be careful not to boil the sauce after adding the coffee, or it will become slightly bitter.

serves 8

1kg very ripe cherry tomatoes,
  stalks removed
1 tsp caster sugar
1 tbsp snipped basil leaves
30ml ruby port
salt and freshly ground pepper
3 tbsp olive oil

60g onions, chopped
80g celery, chopped
6 thick slices of bacon (about 120g),
  derinded and diced
6 drops of Tabasco
1 tsp Worcestershire sauce
juice of ½ lemon

Preheat the oven to 160°C/Gas 3. Put the tomatoes into a shallow casserole or baking dish with a lid and add the sugar, basil, port and a little salt. Cover and cook in the oven for about 45 minutes until the tomatoes have collapsed into a purée.

Meanwhile, put the olive oil into a saucepan and add the onions, celery and bacon. Cook over a medium-low heat for about 20 minutes, stirring frequently, until the vegetables are pale golden and well softened. Spoon off the excess oil, then tip the contents of the saucepan on to the tomatoes.

Transfer the mixture to a blender and whiz for 1 minute, then pass the sauce through a fine-meshed conical sieve into another saucepan. Add the Tabasco, Worcestershire sauce and lemon juice, and season with salt and pepper to taste. Simmer the sauce for another 5 minutes.

Serve immediately, or if preparing ahead, let cool, then store in a sealed container in the fridge for up to 3 days.

This sauce is very versatile and goes with many dishes – pasta, of course, but also with most grilled white meats and vegetables. It can be prepared ahead and reheated very successfully.

blackberry sauce

Fragrant and satisfying, without being overly rich, this sauce
is ideal with roast venison, especially in the autumn.

150g blackberries
30g caster sugar
2 tbsp red wine vinegar
600ml game stock (page 32)
dried zest of ½ orange (see note)
½ cinnamon stick
50ml red wine (preferably Banyuls)
60g butter, chilled and diced
salt and freshly ground pepper

Put the blackberries and sugar into a saucepan and cook over a low heat, stirring
with a wooden spoon until the blackberries have broken down to a purée. Turn
off the heat, add the wine vinegar and give a stir.

Pour in the game stock, add the dried orange zest and cinnamon and bring to
the boil over a medium heat. Lower the heat and simmer gently for 25 minutes,
skimming the surface whenever necessary.

Add the red wine and cook for a further 5 minutes, then pass the sauce through
a fine-meshed conical sieve into a clean saucepan. Whisk in the butter, a little at
a time, then season the sauce with salt and pepper to taste. Serve at once.

NOTE To dry the orange zest, lay the strips on a baking sheet and dry in the oven on its
lowest setting (about 50°C) for about 2 hours. Leave to cool.

This tangy sauce cuts the richness of game terrines or pâtés en croûte perfectly. It is also good served just warm with roast goose.

150g cranberries
75g caster sugar
1 clove, crushed
150g bilberries or blueberries
finely pared zest and juice of 1 lemon

Put the cranberries into a saucepan and add 100ml cold water, the sugar and clove. Bring to a slow simmer and cook gently for 10 minutes.

Add the berries, lemon juice and a further 100ml cold water. Bring back to a simmer and cook gently for another 20 minutes.

In the meantime, blanch the lemon zest in boiling water for 1 minute, then drain and cut into fine julienne.

Keep the sauce at room temperature; it should not be served too cold. If you prefer a very smooth sauce (without any fruit skins), pass it through a fine-meshed conical sieve. Stir the lemon zest into the sauce just before serving.

NOTE The berries in this sauce, particularly bilberries, can be rather tart. If this is the case, add about 30g caster sugar to the sauce halfway through cooking.

onion and green apple chutney

makes about 800g

50ml groundnut oil
400g onions, thinly sliced
120g soft brown sugar
150ml white wine vinegar
1 apple, about 150g (preferably
  Granny Smith), peeled, cored and cut
  into large dice

150g very ripe tomatoes, peeled, deseeded
  and cut into small dice
10 white peppercorns, crushed
½ tsp fine sea salt
1 garlic clove, finely crushed to a purée
½ tsp chilli powder (preferably Espelette)
pinch of ground cinnamon

Heat the groundnut oil in a heavy-based saucepan, add the onions and sweat gently over a low heat for 10 minutes. Add the sugar, increase the heat slightly and cook until the onions are golden and lightly caramelised, stirring every minute or so with a wooden spoon.

Pour in the wine vinegar to deglaze and cook for 3 minutes, then add the remaining ingredients. Cook, stirring frequently, over a gentle heat for about 45 minutes until thick. The chutney is thick enough when a wooden spoon drawn across the bottom of the pan leaves a clear channel for a few seconds.

Pour the chutney into a warm, sterilised preserving jar and seal with a vinegar-proof lid. Store in the fridge for up to 1 month.

I particularly like to eat this chutney with mature Cheddar, barbecued Toulouse sausages and roast pork – hot or cold. In the game season, it is an excellent condiment to serve with leftover pheasant or partridge.

fruity curry sauce

serves 8

40g butter
60g onions, chopped
300g pineapple, cut into small pieces
1 medium banana, cut into rounds
1 dessert apple (preferably Cox's), chopped
40g curry powder, or to taste
2 tbsp grated fresh or desiccated coconut
300ml veal stock (page 26)
200ml coconut milk
salt

Melt the butter in a saucepan, add the onions and sweat them over a low heat for 1 minute to soften slightly. Add the pineapple, banana and apple and cook gently for 5 minutes, stirring with a wooden spoon.

Stir in the curry powder and grated coconut, then pour in the veal stock and coconut milk. Bring to the boil and let bubble gently for 20 minutes.

Pass the sauce through a fine-meshed conical sieve, season with salt to taste and serve immediately. Alternatively, you can keep the sauce warm in a bain-marie; dot the surface with a few flakes of butter to prevent a skin from forming.

Serve this creamy, slightly fruity sauce with grilled veal escalopes or chicken, accompanied by a pilaf or curried rice. Adjust the quantity of curry powder to suit your own taste.

makes about 700g

Make this chutney during the summer, when peaches are at their best.
Serve it with terrines, pâtés and cold meats, especially cold roast chicken.

60g cooking apple, peeled and grated
½ tsp salt
125g very ripe tomatoes, peeled,
  deseeded and chopped
60g onion, finely chopped
finely pared zest of 1 lime, finely
  chopped
juice of the lime
150g caster sugar

½ tsp ground cinnamon
½ tsp ground nutmeg
½ tsp ground white pepper
1 garlic clove, crushed
10g fresh root ginger, finely chopped
150ml white wine vinegar
70g flaked almonds
500g ripe, but firm peaches (preferably
  yellow-fleshed)

Combine all the ingredients except the peaches in a heavy-based saucepan and
bring to the boil over a very low heat, stirring from time to time with a wooden
spoon. Continue to cook for about 30 minutes, giving a stir every 10 minutes, until
the mixture is jam-like and syrupy. Test by running your finger down the back of
the spoon; it should leave a clear trace.

In the meantime, peel the peaches: run the tip of a knife around the circumference,
then immerse in a pan of boiling water. As soon as the skin starts to lift along
the incision, take the peaches out and refresh in iced water. Lift out and pull off
the skin. Halve and stone the peaches, then cut the flesh into cubes.

Add the peaches to the chutney mixture and cook very gently for another
40 minutes, stirring every 10 minutes.

Transfer to a warm, sterilised preserving jar, leave to cool, then seal the jar.
Keep the chutney in the fridge until needed; it will keep for several weeks.

makes about 600g

60g cooking apple, peeled and chopped	150g caster sugar
½ tsp salt	¼ tsp ground cinnamon
125g very ripe tomatoes, peeled,	¼ tsp ground nutmeg
deseeded and chopped	¼ tsp cayenne pepper
60g onion, finely chopped	15g fresh root ginger, finely chopped
60g sultanas	150ml white wine vinegar
1 tbsp orange zest, coarsely chopped	pinch of saffron powder or threads
juice of 1 orange	375g ripe, but firm pears

Combine all the ingredients except the pears in a heavy-based saucepan. Stir and bring to the boil over a very low heat, stirring from time to time with a wooden spoon.

Continue to cook for about 1 hour, giving the mixture a stir every 10 minutes, until it is jam-like and syrupy. Test by running your finger down the back of the spoon; it should leave a clear trace.

In the meantime, peel and core the pears, then cut into small even-sized pieces. Add to the chutney mixture and cook very gently for another 40 minutes, stirring every 10 minutes.

Transfer the chutney to a warm, sterilised preserving jar and leave to cool, then seal the jar. Store in the fridge until needed; it will keep for several weeks.

After making, this chutney is best left for a few days before eating, to allow the flavours to develop. Serve it with cold meats, terrines, pâtés and game, or simply spread on a slice of toast.

Refreshing and brightly coloured, fruit coulis are delectable with a host of different desserts, from simple ice creams and poached fruit to meringues, tarts and soufflés. A coulis may be sweet, mellow or tart, depending on the fruit you use and how ripe it is. When making a coulis you need to find the right level of sweetness, which will be determined partly by what you are serving it with. The less sugar you add, the healthier and more stimulating your coulis will be, but be guided by your taste buds – you don't want it to be so tart that it makes you wince. It is worth noting that a pinch of spice added to a mild coulis will enhance its flavour. And you can prepare ahead if you wish – a coulis will keep for up to a week in a sealed container in the fridge. You will also find a selection of other quick and easy fruit sauces towards the end of this chapter – to accompany ices, fruit, crêpes and various puddings. Most of these have more body than a coulis. I am particularly fond of prune and armagnac sauce (page 260); served with a hot chestnut soufflé it is sublime.

coulis & other fruity dessert sauces

redcurrant and passion frui

Icing sugar gives this coulis a shine and passion fruit seeds add texture and flavour. Serve with poached peaches, vanilla ice cream, parfaits and soufflés.

200g redcurrants
150–200g icing sugar, sifted
1 passion fruit, halved

Whiz for about 2 minutes until you have a smooth redcurrant purée.

Remove the stalks from the redcurrants and tip them into a blender or food processor.

Pour the redcurrant purée into a muslin-lined sieve set over a bowl to strain the juice.

When most of the juice has passed through, gather two corners of the muslin in each hand and twist in opposite directions to extract the remaining juice.

Gradually whisk in the icing sugar – keep tasting the coulis as you add it – the amount you need will depend on the ripeness of the redcurrants.

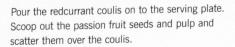

Pour the redcurrant coulis on to the serving plate. Scoop out the passion fruit seeds and pulp and scatter them over the coulis.

stock syrup

makes about 700ml

This basic, light sugar syrup is used to make fruit coulis, which can accompany many different desserts.

400g caster sugar
50g liquid glucose

Combine the sugar, glucose and 350ml water in a saucepan and bring slowly to the boil over a low heat, stirring continuously with a wooden spoon to dissolve the sugar. Boil for 3 minutes, skimming the surface if necessary.

Pass the stock syrup through a fine-meshed conical sieve into a bowl and leave to cool. It will keep in an airtight container in the fridge for up to 2 weeks.

For a heavy stock syrup, to use in a butterscotch sauce (page 292) for example, boil the syrup further until reduced by one-third.

blackberry coulis
Put 350g hulled ripe blackberries, 50ml Kirsch, 150ml stock syrup (left) and the juice of $1/2$ lemon in a blender and whiz for about 1 minute until puréed, then rub through a fine-meshed conical sieve. Delicious served with poached pears, parfaits, iced bombes, or ice creams such as coconut, vanilla or banana. Serves 8

blackcurrant coulis
Put 450g de-stalked blackcurrants in a blender with 150ml stock syrup (left) and the juice of 1 lemon. Process until smooth, then strain through a fine-meshed nylon sieve into a bowl. Taste for sweetness and add extra sugar if necessary. Cover and chill until needed. Delicious with floating islands (poached meringues). Serves 6

redcurrant coulis
Put 350g de-stalked redcurrants in a blender with the juice of 1 lemon and 100ml stock syrup (left) and whiz for 30 seconds, then strain through a fine-meshed conical sieve. This coulis is perfect served with pale-fleshed fruits like peaches and pears, or with vanilla ice cream and iced soufflés. Serves 4

strawberry coulis
Put 500g hulled very ripe strawberries in a blender with 100ml stock syrup (left), the juice of $1/2$ lemon and 10g well-drained bottled green peppercorns for extra bite, if you like. Whiz for 1 minute, then pass the coulis through a fine-meshed conical sieve. Add 10g poppy seeds, if you wish. Serve this coulis with lemon sorbet, vanilla ice cream, poached pears or a pear Charlotte. Marinated thinly sliced raw tuna is also delicious served with this sauce. Serves 8

instant red fruit coulis
Put 100g hulled strawberries and 100g hulled raspberries in a blender with 40g caster sugar, the juice of $1/2$ lemon and 2 tbsp water. Purée for 1 minute, then strain through a fine-meshed conical sieve into a bowl, cover and chill before serving. Serve this fresh-tasting coulis with desserts based on red fruits like strawberries and raspberries. Serves 4

grapefruit coulis with mint

serves 6

This refreshing coulis marries well with blackcurrant sorbet
and orange-based desserts.

2 grapefruits, preferably pink, about 400g each
10g mint leaves, snipped, plus extra to serve
40g caster sugar
150g natural yoghurt
25ml vodka

Using a knife with a flexible blade, peel the grapefruit, removing all pith and
membrane and cut out the segments. Place these in a blender with the mint
and sugar and whiz for 1 minute.

Pass the grapefruit purée through a fine-meshed conical sieve into a large bowl.
Whisk in the yoghurt, then mix in the vodka. Serve chilled.

For an attractive presentation, finely snip a few mint leaves and scatter over
the coulis to serve.

250g tender young rhubarb stalks
100g caster sugar
1 vanilla pod, split lengthways

Cut the rhubarb into small cubes and place in a saucepan with the sugar, vanilla and 100ml water. Slowly bring to the boil and cook gently until the rhubarb is soft enough to crush with a spoon. Take off the heat and remove the vanilla pod.

Tip the rhubarb into a blender and purée for 2 minutes, then pass through a fine-meshed conical sieve into a bowl. If necessary, add a little cold water to thin the coulis. Serve at room temperature to retain its delicate perfume.

This refreshing sauce provides a sharp contrast to a meringue-based vacherin, vanilla bavarois or sweet vanilla ice cream.

serves 6

50g butter
75g caster sugar
500g deseeded red grapes
75ml Armagnac

Melt the butter in a saucepan, stir in the sugar and add the grapes. Cook over a low heat for about 20 minutes, then pour in the Armagnac and ignite it. When the flames have died down, leave the grapes to cool in their syrup for a few minutes.

Put the contents of the pan into a blender and whiz for 30 seconds, then pass through a fine-meshed conical sieve into a bowl. Keep the sauce in a covered container in the fridge until ready to use and give it a stir just before serving.

Make this unusual coulis in late summer, when European grapes are at their best – muscat de Hambourg are my preferred choice. At other times you could use large grapes like Italia, but not seedless grapes as they don't have enough flavour. It enhances the flavour of perfectly ripe figs like a dream.

mango coulis with saffron

serves 6

250g mango flesh, diced
juice of ½ lemon
250ml stock syrup (page 248)
pinch of saffron threads

Put the diced mango into a blender with the lemon juice and all but 2 tbsp of the stock syrup. Whiz the mixture for 2 minutes, then strain the purée through a fine-meshed conical sieve into a bowl.

In a small saucepan, warm the reserved syrup with the saffron threads, then leave to cool. When the syrup is cold, mix it into the mango coulis and chill until ready to serve.

I sometimes serve this fragrant coulis topped with soft poached meringues, as a variation of classic 'floating islands', which uses a base of crème anglaise. You could also serve it with a simple dessert of mango slices and wild strawberries.

Serve this flavourful coulis with an iced vacherin, a medley of red berries, or a simple compote of fresh apricots. It will keep well for several days in a sealed container in the fridge.

3 very ripe pears, about 200g each
pinch of ground cinnamon
100ml red wine (preferably Claret)
150g caster sugar
juice of ½ lemon

Peel and core the pears. Cut them into small pieces and place in a bowl with the cinnamon and red wine. Cover with cling film and leave to marinate for 30 minutes. Drain the pears, reserving the liquor.

Combine the sugar, lemon juice and 2 tbsp water in a heavy-based saucepan. Warm the mixture over a very low heat and let it bubble gently until it becomes a pale caramel.

Take the pan off the heat and pour in the reserved liquor, protecting your hand with a cloth as the mixture may splutter. Stir with a wooden spoon to combine and leave to stand for 5 minutes.

Pour the cooled, diluted caramel over the pears, then transfer to a blender and whiz for 1 minute. Pass the sauce through a fine-meshed conical sieve into a bowl and chill before serving. If it becomes too thick on chilling, dilute with 2–3 tbsp cold water before serving.

serves 6

4 very ripe peaches (preferably white-fleshed)
juice of 1 lemon
4 tbsp lavender honey
1 flowering lavender sprig (optional)

Peel, halve and stone the peaches. Put them in a saucepan with the lemon juice, honey and 150ml water. Slowly bring to a simmer over a low heat and poach gently for 5 minutes. Add the lavender sprig, if using, and cook for a further 30 seconds.

Leave to cool for a few minutes, then transfer the contents of the pan to a blender and whiz for 1 minute.

Pass the sauce through a fine-meshed conical sieve into a bowl and leave to cool completely. When cold, refrigerate until ready to use.

This delectable sauce is superb served with slices of toasted brioche, or simply poured generously over a dish of wild strawberries.

orange butter sauce

serves 6

juice of 6 oranges, about 250g each
100g icing sugar
125g butter, softened

Strain the orange juice through a conical sieve into a heavy-based saucepan and add the icing sugar. Slowly bring to the boil and let bubble over a medium heat until reduced by half.

Turn off the heat and whisk in the softened butter, a little at a time. Serve the sauce at room temperature.

A lovely rich, tangy sauce to serve with crêpes, lemon Charlotte, a warm plum tart or a chocolate soufflé. A few drops of Grand Marnier or Curaçao can be added for extra warmth.

prune and armagnac sauce

serves 10

This sauce is ideal in autumn, served with a prune clafoutis, rice pudding, a hot soufflé of marrons glacés, or pear or banana ice cream.

250g prunes, preferably Agen,
   soaked in cold water for 6 hours
150g caster sugar
½ cinnamon stick
150ml Armagnac
250g butter

Drain the soaked prunes and place them in a saucepan with the sugar and cinnamon. Pour on enough cold water to cover and bring slowly to the boil over a low heat. Simmer for 20 minutes.

Transfer to a bowl, remove the cinnamon stick and leave to cool. Drain the prunes, reserving the cooking liquor, and stone them. Cut 6 prunes into small, even-sized pieces and reserve them in a bowl.

Put the remaining prunes in a shallow pan with the Armagnac, 150ml of the reserved cooking liquor and 100g butter. Heat gently to about 60–70°C; do not allow to boil. Transfer to a blender and whiz for 1 minute.

Tip the prune purée into a saucepan and whisk in the remaining butter, a small piece at a time. Now whisk in enough of the reserved liquor to give the sauce a light ribbon consistency. Add the prune pieces and serve the sauce tepid, or keep it warm in a bain-marie for up to 30 minutes.

serves 8

This sauce will complement a compote of peaches or figs; it is also very good with baked apples.

1 dessert apple, about 100g
2 medium bananas
juice of 1 lemon
50g runny honey
seeds from 2 cardamom pods
100g caster sugar

Peel, core and finely dice the apple. Peel the bananas and slice them into rounds.

Put the prepared fruits into a saucepan with the lemon juice, honey, cardamom seeds, sugar and 200ml water. Slowly bring to the boil over a low heat and simmer very gently for 10 minutes.

Pour the mixture into a blender and whiz for 1 minute, or until you have a very smooth purée. Pass the sauce through a fine-meshed conical sieve into a bowl and leave to cool. Once cold, refrigerate until ready to use.

banana sauce

serves 8

2 medium bananas
juice of 1 lemon
350g caster sugar
200g crème fraîche
100ml white rum
150ml milk

Peel the bananas, slice into rounds and immediately toss with the lemon juice to stop them discolouring.

Dissolve the sugar in 150ml water in a heavy-based saucepan over a low heat, then bring to the boil and cook to a pale caramel. Take off the heat and add all the other ingredients, mixing gently with a spatula.

Return the pan to a medium heat and cook at a gentle bubble for about 20 minutes, delicately stirring the mixture frequently.

Leave the sauce to cool slightly, then transfer to a blender and whiz for 1 minute. Pass the sauce through a fine-meshed conical sieve into a bowl and keep it in the fridge until ready to use.

With its Caribbean flavour, this simple sauce is a perfect accompaniment to a dish of exotic fruits.

hot apricot sauce

This sauce is excellent served with baked apples, exotic fruit soufflés and ice creams flavoured with nuts such as almonds and walnuts.

300g very ripe apricots
75g caster sugar
1 tbsp finely snipped mint leaves
1 tbsp Kirsch (optional)

Halve the apricots and remove the stones. Put the fruit into a saucepan with the sugar and 200ml water. Slowly bring to a simmer and cook gently for about 10 minutes until tender. The timing will depend on the ripeness of the apricots.

Transfer the mixture to a blender and purée for 1 minute, then pass the sauce through a fine-meshed conical sieve into a bowl. Add the snipped mint and Kirsch, if you like. Serve the sauce hot so that it retains its wonderful aroma.

20g sultanas
300ml double cream
60g caster sugar
2 tsp cornflour, blended with 2 tbsp milk
75ml dark rum (preferably Captain Morgan
   or Negrita)

Blanch the sultanas in boiling water for 1 minute, refresh in cold water, then drain well.

Put the cream and sugar into a small saucepan and bring to the boil over a low heat. Add the blended cornflour, stirring as you go, and cook, stirring, for 2 minutes.

Pour in the rum and simmer the sauce for another 2 minutes, then stir in the sultanas and serve piping hot.

The perfect complement to bread and butter pudding, Christmas pudding and rum and raisin ice cream.

serves 8

500ml red wine (preferably Pinot Noir)
200g caster sugar
1 cinnamon stick, crushed
1 clove
2 vanilla pods, split lengthways
finely pared zest and juice of 1 orange
small pinch of freshly grated nutmeg
1 tbsp mint leaves

Pour the red wine into a saucepan and add the sugar, spices, vanilla and orange zest and juice. Slowly bring to the boil and let bubble gently until the liquid has reduced by one-third.

Off the heat, add the nutmeg and mint and allow to infuse for a few minutes, then pass the sauce through a fine-meshed conical sieve into a bowl. Leave to cool completely, then refrigerate until ready to use.

I serve this sauce with poached peaches or pears, or to enhance the flavour of a moulded rice pudding. You can also churn the sauce to make an excellent sorbet; just stir in 75ml water before churning.

Crème anglaise is without doubt the queen of dessert sauces. This classic, elegant custard has stood the test of time – the recipe I am sharing with you is the one I have used for the past 50 years! Made to perfection, it is velvety smooth, glossy and silky, rich and creamy, yet delicately flavoured and it has a lovely, long finish in the mouth. To guide you to success, follow the step-by-step photographs overleaf. The amount of sugar can be adjusted slightly if you like – for a less sweet custard, you can reduce the sugar by 10% without adversely affecting the final texture. Sabayons are another group of very refined dessert sauces, with a wonderful light, airy quality. Patient whisking, on and off the heat, gives these sauces their characteristic billowy texture. Related to the family of emulsion sauces, they do not benefit from sitting around, so be ready to serve them soon after whisking to enjoy them at their best. I love them all, and in particular the lemon grass and thyme sabayon (on page 279). Clean and fresh tasting, it slips down very easily, as I am sure you will discover…

custards & sabayons

crème anglaise

The perfect accompaniment to so many desserts, this classic light, creamy custard can be flavoured to taste (see overleaf).

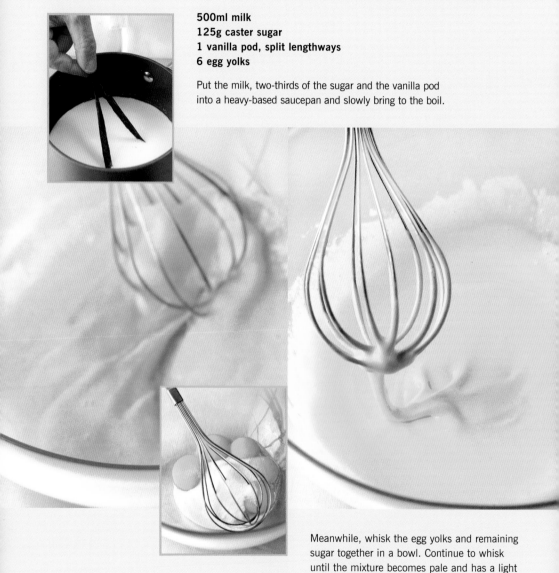

500ml milk
125g caster sugar
1 vanilla pod, split lengthways
6 egg yolks

Put the milk, two-thirds of the sugar and the vanilla pod into a heavy-based saucepan and slowly bring to the boil.

Meanwhile, whisk the egg yolks and remaining sugar together in a bowl. Continue to whisk until the mixture becomes pale and has a light ribbon consistency.

Cook over a low heat, stirring with a wooden spatula or spoon; do not let it boil or it may curdle. The custard is ready when it has thickened slightly – just enough to lightly coat the back of the spatula. When you run your finger through, it should leave a clear trace. Immediately take the pan off the heat.

Unless you are serving the crème anglaise warm, pour through a fine-meshed conical sieve into a bowl set over crushed ice and leave to cool, stirring occasionally to prevent a skin from forming.

Pour the boiling milk on to the egg yolks, whisking continuously, then pour the mixture back into the saucepan.

The custard will keep in a covered container in the fridge for up to 48 hours.

pistachio crème anglaise
Either use 40g pistachio paste or 200g skinned fresh pistachio nuts soaked in cold water for 24 hours, drained and crushed to a paste using a pestle and mortar. Pour one-third of the hot crème anglaise on to the pistachio paste, stirring with a whisk, then stir into the rest of the hot custard. Whiz in a blender for about 3 minutes until very smooth. Pass through a fine-meshed conical sieve into a bowl, cool over crushed ice and chill until ready to use. This unusual custard is superb with poached white peaches and pears poached in Sauternes. Makes about 750ml

chocolate crème anglaise
Stir 60g melted good-quality bitter chocolate into the milk as you warm it. Serve with banana splits. Makes about 750ml

coffee crème anglaise
Stir 1 tbsp instant coffee powder into the hot milk. This is particularly good served with meringues. Makes about 750ml

ginger crème anglaise
Infuse the milk with 20g peeled and finely sliced fresh root ginger rather than vanilla. Try serving with lightly poached (and well drained) rhubarb. Makes about 750ml

spiced crème anglaise
Infuse the milk with 4 or 5 star anise instead of vanilla. This fragrant custard is delicious served with spiced baked apples. Makes about 750ml

minted crème anglaise
Infuse the milk with a bunch of fresh mint rather than vanilla. The freshness of this mint-flavoured custard goes brilliantly with all berries. It is also excellent with chocolate ice cream and chocolate truffle cake. Makes about 750ml

lemon custard

serves 4

240ml single cream
140g caster sugar (plus extra if the lemons
   are very tart)
240ml lemon juice (from about 6 lemons)
6 egg yolks

Combine the cream, 60g sugar and the lemon juice in a saucepan and slowly bring
to the boil over a low heat.

Meanwhile, in a bowl, whisk the egg yolks with the remaining 80g sugar to a ribbon
consistency. Pour the boiling cream on to the egg mixture, whisking continuously.

Pour the custard back into the saucepan and cook very gently for 2 minutes, stirring
continuously with a wooden spoon or spatula; don't let it boil or it may curdle.

Pass the custard through a fine-meshed conical sieve into a chilled bowl. Leave to
cool, stirring occasionally to prevent a skin from forming. When the custard
is cold, cover the bowl with cling film and refrigerate until ready to serve.

Served with red fruits – like strawberries, raspberries,
redcurrants and blackcurrants – this sharp lemony custard makes
the perfect summer dessert. To accentuate the flavour, sprinkle
on some shreds of candied lemon zest just before serving.

serves 4

This delectable sauce is based on a recipe of the late, great chef Alain Chapel. It is especially delicious served with a slice of freshly grilled brioche, sprinkled with a veil of icing sugar.

120ml milk
750ml whipping cream
3 tbsp jasmine tea leaves
8 egg yolks
150g soft brown sugar

Pour 100ml milk and 250ml cream into a small saucepan and slowly bring to the boil. Immediately take the pan off the heat and stir in the tea leaves. Cover the pan and leave to infuse for 2 minutes.

Meanwhile, put the egg yolks and brown sugar into a bowl and work together lightly with a wooden spoon for about 1 minute.

Pour the hot infusion on to the egg mixture and mix thoroughly. Stir in the remaining cream and set aside to infuse for 30 minutes.

Pass the mixture through a fine-meshed conical sieve into a clean saucepan and cook very gently for about 5 minutes, stirring continuously with a wooden spoon. Pour into a bowl and stir in the remaining milk. Leave to cool, stirring occasionally to prevent a skin from forming. Cover and chill until ready to serve.

classic sabayon

serves 4

You will need a cooking thermometer to check the temperature of the sabayon.

100ml Sauternes or other sweet white wine
3 egg yolks
40g caster sugar

Two-thirds fill a saucepan (large enough to hold a heatproof round-bottomed bowl) with warm water, and heat gently. Pour the Sauternes into the bowl, then add the egg yolks, whisking as you go. Carry on whisking as you shower in the sugar.

Place the bowl over the saucepan, making sure that the bottom of the bowl is not in direct contact with the water. Continue whisking the mixture over the heat so that it gradually thickens, making sure that the temperature of the water in the pan increases steadily but moderately.

Turn off the heat and continue whisking until the sabayon has a very thick ribbon consistency and a fluffy, rich and shiny texture. Remove the bowl from the pan.

After 8–10 minutes, the mixture should have reached a light ribbon consistency. It is essential to keep whisking all the time. When the temperature reaches 55°C, the sabayon is cooked.

Serve the sabayon immediately – either in glasses just as it is, or spoon it over a dessert such as a medley of red fruits or fruit-filled crêpes in a gratin dish and place under a hot grill until the sabayon is lightly browned.

marsala sabayon
For a richer sabayon, replace the Sauternes with Marsala, or Banyuls if you prefer. This is particularly delicious spooned over summer berries and briefly gratinéed – either under the grill or using a cook's blowtorch. Serves 4

eau-de-vie sabayon
Replace the Sauternes with 75ml eau-de-vie, such as raspberry or pear, or Kirsch, and 50ml water. Add an extra 20g sugar. Serves 4

lemon grass and thyme sabayon
Bring 750ml water to the boil in a saucepan. Add 1 roughly chopped, bruised lemon grass stalk, 1 small thyme sprig and 4 kaffir lime leaves, and simmer, covered, for 2 minutes. Strain through a muslin-lined sieve into a heatproof bowl, pressing with the back of a small ladle to extract as much flavour as possible from the lemon grass. Set the bowl over a pan half-filled with tepid water. Add 6 egg yolks, 75g caster sugar and the juice of 1 lime. Place over a medium heat and whisk constantly with a balloon whisk for 10–12 minutes until the sabayon is cooked (see page 277); do not overheat. It is ready when it is rich, shiny and fluffy and has the consistency of half-beaten egg whites. Serve immediately, sprinkled with lime zest. Serves 4

serves 4

> I like to serve this sabayon as a dessert in itself with lacy orange tuiles for contrast, but it also makes a tempting sauce to serve with fresh orange segments or poached pears, drained of their syrup.

1 tbsp instant coffee
4 egg yolks
50g caster sugar
½ tsp ground cinnamon

For your bain-marie, half-fill a saucepan large enough to hold a round-bottomed copper bowl or heatproof glass bowl with warm water. Place the pan over a low heat.

Put the coffee and 4 tbsp cold water into the bowl and whisk with a balloon whisk to dissolve. Lightly whisk in the egg yolks, sugar and cinnamon.

Set the bowl in the bain-marie and whisk continuously for 10–12 minutes. The mixture will thicken and increase dramatically in volume as air is incorporated.

The sabayon is ready when it is light, fluffy and shiny, and thick enough to leave a dense ribbon when the whisk is lifted. The water in the bain-marie must not exceed 90°C and the temperature of the sabayon itself must not go above 65°C. If necessary, turn off or lower the heat as you whisk.

As soon as the sabayon is ready, stop whisking, spoon into glasses or a sauceboat and serve immediately.

coffee sabayon with tia maria
Dissolve the coffee in 3 tbsp water only. In place of the cinnamon, add 50ml Tia Maria or Kahlua liqueur along with the sugar and egg yolks.

caramel sabayon

serves 4

100g caster sugar
120ml double cream
4 egg yolks
juice of 1 lemon

In a medium heavy-based saucepan, heat the sugar until it begins to liquefy and darken. Stir with a wooden spoon until the caramel is clear and the colour of runny honey. Immediately remove the pan from the heat.

Standing well back and protecting your hand with a cloth, add the cream to the caramel. It will spit and bubble vigorously for a few seconds. When the bubbling subsides, stir and reheat gently until the caramel has completely dissolved and the cream is smooth. Leave to cool completely.

Put the egg yolks into a clean saucepan and add the cooled caramel cream, then the lemon juice. Set over a very low heat and whisk together. As soon as the sabayon reaches 60°C, take the pan off the heat. Use the sabayon immediately.

Macerate tropical fruits in white rum, scatter in a gratin dish, top with this sabayon and flash under a hot grill or use a cook's blowtorch to tinge the sauce with colour for an easy dessert.

serves 6

This sauce has an unusual but delicious flavour, which
perfectly complements a pear tart, plum clafoutis, pistachio ice
cream or compote of yellow peaches.

250ml milk
60g caster sugar
25g liquorice extract, or 50g liquorice sticks,
   cut into small pieces
3 egg yolks
50ml whipping cream

Put the milk into a saucepan with two-thirds of the sugar, add the liquorice and
bring to the boil over a medium heat.

Meanwhile, whisk the egg yolks and remaining sugar together in a bowl until the
mixture becomes pale and has a light ribbon consistency.

Pour the liquorice milk on to the egg yolk and sugar mixture, whisking constantly,
then pour the mixture back into the saucepan.

Cook over a low heat, stirring with a wooden spatula or spoon; do not let it boil
or it may curdle. The sauce is ready when it has thickened enough to lightly coat
the back of the spatula. When you run your finger through, it should leave a clear
trace. Immediately take the pan off the heat.

Pour the sauce through a fine-meshed conical sieve into a bowl set over crushed
ice and leave to cool, stirring occasionally to prevent a skin from forming. (At this
stage, the sauce can be kept covered in the fridge for up to 48 hours.)

Just before serving, whip the cream until floppy and fold into the sauce.

Smooth, velvety rich and decadent, chocolate sauce is immensely popular with all ages. The classic partner to poached pears, profiteroles and vanilla ice cream, it is also delicious with meringues, crêpes and certain flavoured ice creams, such as coffee, pistachio and banana. For optimum results, it is important to use a good-quality chocolate, such as Valrhona, with a minimum of 70% cocoa solids for a dark chocolate sauce. Similarly, if you are using white chocolate, buy white couverture or best quality chocolate, otherwise the result will be disappointing. For a chocolate sauce to have a perfect, smooth-flowing, palate-pleasing consistency, it should be served warm rather than hot (between 30 and 40°C). A dash of liqueur, such as Grand Marnier, will add a sweet spirituous touch. Of the other rich, indulgent sauces for desserts, caramel and butterscotch are my favourites. Again, you can serve these with ice creams, though they are probably best appreciated with steamed puddings, baked Charlottes or poached pears in winter when heartier desserts are appreciated. I advise you, however, not to overindulge with these, because they are genuinely rich!

chocolate & other rich creamy sauces

classic rich chocolate sauce

This rich, velvety sauce is sublime spooned over vanilla or coffee ice cream,
poached pears, profiteroles or meringues filled with whipped cream.

200g good-quality dark bitter chocolate,
   70% cocoa solids (preferably Valrhona)
175ml milk
2 tbsp double cream
30g caster sugar
30g butter, diced

Combine the milk, cream and sugar in a
saucepan, stir with a whisk and bring to the boil.

Chop the chocolate and place in a heatproof bowl.
Set over a pan of gently simmering water and
allow to melt slowly, stirring occasionally until very
smooth. Take off the heat.

Turn off the heat and whisk in the butter, a little at a time, to give a smooth, homogeneous sauce. Pass it through a fine-meshed conical sieve. Serve at once or keep warm in a bain-marie until needed.

Still stirring with the whisk, pour the boiling milk mixture on to the melted chocolate, then return the mixture to the pan and let it bubble over the heat for a few seconds, stirring continuously.

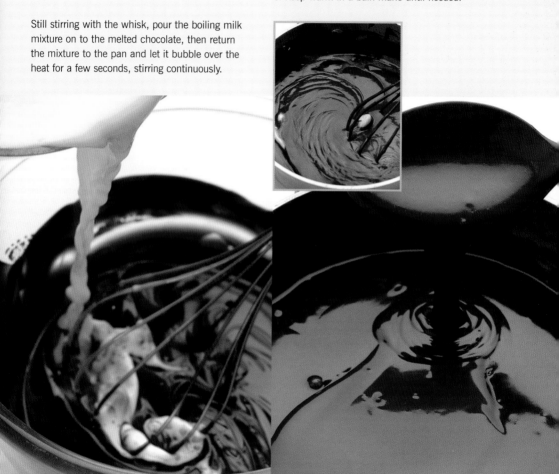

Try adding a dash of Grand Marnier to enhance the sauce, or infuse the creamy milk mixture with a good pinch of crushed cardamom seeds for a light spicy note.

white chocolate sauce with mint

serves 6

Mint adds a touch of freshness to this sauce, which is sublime poured over dark chocolate ice cream and scattered with a few pistachios.

250g best-quality white chocolate or
   white couverture
100ml milk
250ml double cream
7g fresh mint leaves
3/4 tsp caraway seeds

Chop the white chocolate and place it in a heatproof bowl. Set over a pan of barely simmering water (making sure the bottom of the bowl is not in contact with the water) and melt it gently over a low heat, stirring with a wooden spoon occasionally until smooth.

Meanwhile, bring the milk and cream to the boil in a saucepan. When it begins to bubble, toss in the mint leaves and caraway seeds, turn off the heat and cover the pan. Leave to infuse for 10 minutes.

As soon as the chocolate has melted, remove the bowl from the heat. Pass the infused cream mixture through a fine-meshed conical sieve on to the melted chocolate, mixing with a whisk until thoroughly amalgamated.

Transfer the chocolate sauce to a clean saucepan set over a medium heat and let bubble for a few seconds, whisking continuously.

Serve the sauce immediately, or you can keep it warm in a bain-marie for a short while if necessary.

quick chocolate sauce

serves 6

Perfect for impatient cooks, this sauce can be prepared in a trice. It is ideal for serving with pancakes, waffles or vanilla ice cream. To enhance the flavour, I like to infuse some basil leaves in the cream.

**250g good-quality dark bitter chocolate,
   70% cocoa solids (preferably Valrhona)
300ml single cream
1 tbsp basil leaves (optional)**

Chop the chocolate into small, even-sized pieces. Pour the cream into a saucepan and add the basil leaves, if using. Heat until just beginning to bubble, then add the chocolate, stirring with a whisk.

Reduce the heat to low and cook gently until the sauce is smooth and unctuous.

Pour into a jug or strain through a fine-meshed conical sieve to remove the basil leaves, if using. Serve immediately.

serves 6

200ml maple syrup
1 tbsp instant coffee, dissolved in 1 tbsp
   hot water
50ml vodka
50ml Drambuie
8 coffee beans, coarsely crushed

Warm the maple syrup in a small saucepan, then add the dissolved coffee.
As soon as the syrup is hot but not boiling, take the pan off the heat and lightly
whisk in the vodka and Drambuie.

Cover the sauce with cling film and set aside to cool.

Stir in the crushed coffee beans just before serving.

This irresistible, iridescent sauce is delicious served with
a vanilla and praline parfait or with warm waffles. The alcohol adds an
agreeable aroma, which is particularly inviting on a cold wintry day.

butterscotch sauce

Serve this rich sauce with vanilla ice cream or a steamed pudding, or an apple dessert such as apple Charlotte.

400ml single cream
120ml cane sugar syrup, or heavy stock syrup
  (page 248)
75g caster sugar
1 vanilla pod
60g unsalted or slightly salted butter, diced

Pour the cream into a heavy-based saucepan and add the sugar syrup and sugar. Split the vanilla pod lengthways, scrape out the seeds with the tip of a knife and add them to the pan. Slowly bring to the boil, stirring.

Let the mixture bubble gently, stirring continuously with a small whisk, until it is the colour of pale hazelnuts.

Stir in the butter, a little at a time, until completely amalgamated and unctuous. Serve piping hot.

serves 6

100g caster sugar
75g butter, softened
1 vanilla pod
400ml double cream

Combine the sugar and butter in a heavy-based saucepan. Split the vanilla pod lengthways, scrape out the seeds with the tip of a knife and add them to the pan. Set over a very low heat and stir continuously with a wooden spoon until the sugar has dissolved completely.

Continue to cook until the mixture turns an attractive caramel colour. Immediately take the pan off the heat and stir in the cream, protecting your hand with a cloth as the mixture may splutter. Mix well to combine.

Return to a medium heat and cook the sauce for 5 minutes, stirring continuously with the wooden spoon. The sauce should be perfectly blended, smooth and shiny. Pass it through a fine-meshed conical sieve and leave to cool.

Serve the sauce once it has cooled, or store in a sealed container in the fridge for up to 3 days.

This simple sauce is delectable drizzled over poached pears or pancakes, or try stirring it into natural yoghurt.

A guide to selecting sauces to partner whatever you are planning
to prepare and cook.

rouille, 100

spinach
chicken gravy with thyme, 201
fresh tomato and basil coulis, 164
Parmesan vinaigrette, 112

steak
béarnaise sauce, 98
foie gras butter, 128
juniper sauce, 219

strawberries
coulis of peaches with lavender honey, 257
lemon custard, 274
minted crème anglaise, 273

summer berries
coulis of peaches with lavender honey, 257
lemon custard, 274
sabayons 276–279

sweetbreads
albufera sauce, 66
allemande sauce, 74
caper sauce with anchovies, 78
sauce suprême with sherry and mushrooms, 70
velouté sauce, 66

swordfish
pineapple salsa with coriander, 142

toast canapés
anchovy butter, 126
foie gras butter, 128
langoustine butter, 132
red pepper butter, 133
red pepper salsa, 136
Roquefort butter, 128
shrimp butter, 131

tomatoes
bagnarotte sauce, 85

tongue
albufera sauce, 66
allemande sauce, 74
minted sauce suprême, 68
rémoulade sauce, 85

trout
bois boudran sauce, 147
matelote sauce, 173

tuna
Claret sauce, 176
ginger and chilli sauce for sashimi, 150
herb salsa, 138
strawberry coulis, 249

turbot
américaine sauce, 192
beer sauce, 79
Champagne beurre blanc, 103
Champagne sauce, 174
cider beurre blanc, 104
leek coulis with saffron and dill, 158
Sauternes sauce with pistachios, 178
seaspray sauce, 184
Vincent sauce, 93

turkey
aurora sauce, 58
bread sauce, 65
buccaneer's sauce, 204
paprika butter, 133
spiced marinade for poultry, 43

vacherin
coulis of pears with red wine, 255

veal
aubergine sauce with tarragon, 217
buccaneer's sauce, 204
cep coulis, 165
chasseur sauce, 206
fruity curry sauce, 240
five-spice sauce, 213
goat's cheese butter, 128

paprika butter, 133
parsley coulis, 167
sauce Albert, 75
sauce suprême with sherry and mushrooms, 70
soubise sauce, 58
tomato and basil salsa, 141
zingara sauce, 212

vegetable lasagne
asparagus coulis, 156

vegetables
aïoli, 87
flavoured butters, 126–8
raspberry vinegar, 119
mornay sauce, 60
sauce balkanaise, 89
tomato water, 46
yoghurt sauce, 148
see also crudités and individual types of vegetable

venison
blackberry sauce, 236
cooked red wine marinade for meat and game, 41
game stock, 32
juniper sauce, 219
mushroom and horseradish nage, 50
port sauce, 229

waffles
maple syrup, coffee and Drambuie sauce, 291
quick chocolate sauce, 290

whiting
aromatic herb infusion, 48
matelote sauce, 173

wild boar
apple sauce, 224
pumpkin sauce with sweet spices, 232

yoghurt
caramel sauce, 293

acknowledgements

No book is the work of a single author. Each member of my team below is an ingredient in the final result and I offer my thanks to them:
Alain Roux, my son, Chef Patron and **Michael Nizzero**, First Sous Chef for their relentless testing and presentation during the photo sessions.
Martin Brigdale who has brought to the page my dreams for this book. His step-by-step photography is superb and the finished sauces edible. His stable temperament was oil on my troubled waters.
Mary Evans has an eye that can see through a needle. Her goal of achievement for this book never wavered and her ability to achieve this end was never in question.

Janet Illsley, as the fine editor she is, managed to coax me that less is more without my realising that 'I was gently being manipulated'.
Sally Somers joined the team mid-translation, when she replaced Kate Whiteman. For a first-time collaboration her work was a revelation and her marvellous job gave life to my sauces.
Claude Grant has typed all 11 manuscripts and this last one was almost one too many. She applied herself with the same loyalty and vigour that she always gives and I thank her for it.
Robyn Roux, my wife, who read and checked my recipes, even those that I actually stole from her.

This book is dedicated to **Kate Whiteman**. Sadly, we tragically lost Kate in early 2009 and I miss her very much. We first met in 1983 when she translated my first book, New Classic Cuisine. Over the following 24 years, Kate translated a further 10 titles, which naturally changed our relationship from collaborators to friends. Kate was an author in her own right so I was always grateful when she accepted another project.